IN THE SHADOW
OF
THE CROSS

Ellen,

Thanks for your support

Charles

IN THE SHADOW OF THE CROSS

The True Account of My Childhood
Sexual and Ritual Abuse at the Hands of
a Roman Catholic Priest

Charles L. Bailey, Jr.

Commentary by Susan Currier Bailey

iUniverse, Inc.
New York Lincoln Shanghai

In the Shadow of the Cross
The True Account of My Childhood Sexual and Ritual Abuse at the Hands of a Roman Catholic Priest

iUniverse books may be ordered through booksellers or by contacting:

iUniverse
2021 Pine Lake Road, Suite 100
Lincoln, NE 68512
www.iuniverse.com
1-800-Authors (1-800-288-4677)

The views expressed in this work are solely those of the author and do not necessarily reflect the views of the publisher, and the publisher hereby disclaims any responsibility for them.

ISBN-13: 978-0-595-40578-7 (pbk)
ISBN-13: 978-0-595-84944-4 (ebk)
ISBN-10: 0-595-40578-9 (pbk)
ISBN-10: 0-595-84944-X (ebk)

Printed in the United States of America

To my best friend, my wife, my soul mate, Sue (formerly Susan Currier). Without her unfailing support, I could not have gotten to this point. She has been the best wife a man could ever be blessed with, and she truly loves me unconditionally.

To my children, their spouses, and grandchildren. I gratefully acknowledge their love and support.

To my doctor, Stephen Driscoll, PhD, who knew all the right things to say and how to say them. He is a consummate professional.

CONTENTS

FOREWORD

Charles Bailey speaks from the depths of his soul about the vile assaults inflicted on him by an evil man cloaked in a disguise of goodness. He discovers, forty years later, that what he thought was his singular hell was also experienced by thousands of others at the hands of similarly evil men. The ultimate in evil is the assault on a child's innocence while confusing his young mind by claiming authority derived from God, in an attempt to turn vile, evil violations into sanctimonious acts of religious sacrifice. These heinous deeds robbed children of their innocence and safety and made them feel dirty and unworthy of God's or anyone else's love. The children were then discarded like vessels used-up for the pleasure of their perpetrators, who would then slither on to their next innocent victims.

Bailey's courage in publicly describing his experience has unmasked an equally and perhaps even greater evil: the conspiracy perpetrated by the Catholic Church to protect these evildoers. The Church rescues them from one location and transplants them to another, where they set forth preying on new victims. Just as the evil priests manipulate their victims' minds, the Church carries this exploitation to the level of organizational deception by maintaining the anonymity of the predators and by "paying off" some victims of their assaults in return for secrecy and for not prosecuting the evildoers. The church continues to endorse the priests as upstanding, blessed men to be trusted by the congregations to which they are subsequently assigned, and then the priests repeat their terrible crimes again and again.

Bailey implicitly raises the question of whether the Catholic Church as an organization is corrupt or whether the thousands of abusive priests are misrepresentative exceptions. This concern is observed in his interactions with the local bishop who appears to be genuinely compassionate with Bailey's experience while simultaneously trying to protect his church from expanded scandal by keeping secret the names of his priests who have been identified with errant behavior. The cover-up versus the purgative approach to this moral cancer is troubling, and Bailey's account describes his discouragement as he battles against overwhelming odds. He perseveres by trying to help one person at a time. He has become the go-to guy in his community as a person who survived the "victim hood" of these crimes. He represents the hope that people can recover and go on to lead healthy lives with family, friends, and most important, themselves.

Bailey describes the "collateral damage" that ensues, including the disruption of relationships with some family members who he thought would be his allies, the struggle with the loss of both his religious faith and the trust of clergy representatives, and the attempt to understand why this wickedness had happened to him. *Am I that despicable in God's eyes?* He wonders. *Does God not care? Is he just not available? Or maybe he just does not exist.* People who read this book, who have suffered sexual abuse, might see themselves in Bailey's accounting of his perilous and ultimately triumphant journey. It is gut-wrenching to read the horrors that one human can impose on another. It is made all the more vicious by an adult corrupting the body, mind, and soul of a child while masquerading in a uniform that is associated with God, goodness, and moral leadership. Bailey's ultimate confrontation with secrets that he was commanded to keep and with his feelings of shame, misguided though they were, are bound to inspire all who have been in that dark, lonely, painful place. Bailey's story is evidence that good can overcome evil and that one can return from the depths of a personal hell to rise again and live a good and productive life. He demonstrates in his daily life that the human spirit is ultimately resilient and can transform adversity into beneficial outcomes. It is a privilege to come to know and work with him. My life, perspectives, and understanding have been opened and expanded by his. His story reminds us that life's painful experiences challenge and test us, and, in so doing, they make us stronger. Perhaps it is not the answers that we attain about life but rather the questions that we dare to ask, ponder, and live with that help us to become ultimately human.

Stephen Driscoll, PhD

PREFACE

Why write this book? Why read this book? Why now? Those might be just some of the questions running through your head as you thumb through this book. However, remember the adage "don't judge a book by its cover"? Well, this is one of those books. As you read this book, you will see the significance of the title, but I'm not giving it away here, not yet. This book was written for the protection of all children—yours, mine, and those yet to come into this challenging world of ours. It was written to enlighten both mothers and fathers of children who have been sexually abused by clergy, so they can truly understand the effects of this abuse on their children. Reading this book will give parents the much needed insight to help both themselves and their child through the hurt. It will educate parents on how their children might feel about themselves, their siblings, and God, as a result of the abuse.

Writing this book is like standing in public naked. You will see and feel why this is, as my account unfolds before you. I am bared down to my very soul, my very essence. However, if I do not approach this topic head-on, no one will truly understand the pain and anguish that a child can experience at the hands of someone he believed was holy. Also, if only one person, one child, is saved from this evil, then writing this book was worthwhile. My hope is that people will read this book and come away with the understanding that sexual abuse truly rapes an entire family, because the family receives collateral damage from the abuse.

The journey from innocent to victim lasts for a microsecond, but to go from victim to survivor takes years. In my case, the abuse experience, which began at age ten, was hidden from all but myself for forty-plus years, and only after more than three years of professional help have I begun to believe that the abuse wasn't my fault. Other victims, sadly, never get to the survivor stage, and some even end their lives at an early age.

Imagine being ten years old, standing in front of a mirror, and seeing yourself clearly and completely in focus. Then, in a split second, your abuser smashes your self-image to pieces. You lose yourself to a pile of pieces with sharp, jagged edges. You no longer exist as the ten-year-old innocent. The time you spend rebuilding yourself is not unlike trying to reassemble a broken mirror. You get cut by every piece you put back together, all the while hurting like no one should hurt. As time passes, you "complete" the reassembly of that mirror, but the image is forever damaged, distorted. Some pieces are still missing; your vision of yourself is never quite as clear as it was as a child. You are forever changed. Will the repair hold up over time? Will you lose the love of family members when they learn of your past? Sadly, that is sometimes true.

I feel that I see things differently from others. I feel that much of what I see is distorted by the crack marks on my "mirror." However, Dr. Driscoll, my psychologist, tells me I see things more clearly than almost anyone. He says that I have greater insight and clarity than most.

It will be a tough read for you, as the unfiltered truth is sometimes a hard swallow. You will feel a range of emotions, but—know this—it is all true. This is a personal account of my childhood sexual abuse at the hands of a Holy Roman Catholic Priest. It is not *based* on fact; rather, it *is* fact. All of the content is true, and some of it is horrifying.

ACKNOWLEDGMENTS

My thanks to A. W. Richard Sipe for his permission to quote the following from his book *Celibacy in Crisis: A Secret World Revisited* and for his support.

> A. W. Richard Sipe has been on a mission to bring the problems surrounding clerical celibacy and sexuality to light since the publication of his groundbreaking books, *A Secret World* (1990), and *Sex, Priests, and Power* (1995). Spending eighteen years in a Benedictine monastery, with eleven of those years active in the priesthood, he was trained to deal with the mental health problems of Catholic priests and the religious. In tandem with practicing psychotherapy, teaching in major seminaries, and lecturing in a medical school, he conducted a twenty-five-year ethnographic study of celibacy and sexuality in the priesthood. He has served as a consultant and expert witness on more than 150 cases of sexual abuse of minors by priests. Currently retired from his psychotherapy practice and living in California, he continues to write and lecture on clerical celibacy. His work with clerical sexuality has attracted worldwide attention. He has been interviewed in numerous publications, including *Time, Newsweek, The New Yorker,* and has been featured on hundreds of national and local radio programs. He is engaged with Sony pictures in preparing a film on clerical sexual abuse.

Thanks to Pastor Steve Matthews for his help in closing the gap between myself and God.

Many thanks to John Aretakis, attorney; he works tirelessly and fearlessly to help end this tragedy. He defends us like no one else does. His wife and child embrace his mission and allow John to be available day and night, weekends included. John is one amazing man. He truly cares.

Web site credit goes to my son, Charles L. Bailey, III. Chas, as he is called, designed, built, and maintains this resource for all of us (www.intheshadowofthecross.net). Please visit this site.
It will be worth your time.

Special thanks go to Barbara Blaine, David Clohessy, and Barbara Dorris; their extensive work, help, and continuing support make SNAP a reality. (www.snapnetwork.org) (Survivors Network of those Abused by Priests)

Many thanks to Barbara O'Brien for her constructive review of my manuscript.

I must also give heartfelt thanks to Rachele Walter, my PSA (Publishing Services Associate) at iUniverse.com whose support helped me through this process and never wavered, no matter how high the mountain before us seemed.

1

DEAR GOD

Me, shortly before the abuse started.

Dear God, are you there? Hello, Hello?

As I sit here at my computer typing this, I am a fifty-three-year-old man, but I am also a ten-year-old boy, grasping for truth, understanding, and most of all help. What is happening?

Dear God, are you there? This is Charles Bailey. I am ten years old. Hello? Hello? Do you hear me? What am I saying? You're God, so of course you know me. You see all and know all. I was taught that in Holy Family School, in third and fourth grade. A man in priestly robes has just raped me. Is he one of yours? I can't believe he is one of yours. How could you let this happen? Do you not love me? I pray that I am not too dirty now for your love. I know that my soul has

1

been blackened by this man in priestly garb. I sit on my bed and look at the crucifix with your body nailed to it. I hurt too, God. So very, very much. Can you help me? Will you help me? Please stop this man from hurting me. Can you give him a stroke? A heart attack? A car wreck? If you can't, please remove me from this Earth, as soon as possible. I would take my life in an instant if I didn't think that I would be put into Hell for all eternity. Maybe when I am up on the garage roof in one of my hiding places in the little nook by the chimney, I could accidentally fall? Would you still make me burn in Hell for all eternity? Since you know all, you would know it truly wasn't an accident. How about if I fall off the back porch roof after shoveling the snow off? That would be an accident, wouldn't it? I'll try. The pile of snow is many feet tall. It's almost up to the edge of the roof, but if I run a little to the left, everyone would think I just goofed and hit the sidewalk and killed myself accidentally. Ah, but you would still know God, wouldn't you? Maybe not. Here I go, running along the roof. As I become airborne, my siblings yell. I know it will be over soon, any second. I hit the sidewalk. But I'm still here; my winter clothes were so thick and padded that I am only bruised, and only a little. Should I do it again? This time I'll lead with my head. That would surely work. Death—finally pain free. Even if you send me to Hell, God, then at least Father Thomas Neary couldn't get to me anymore. It's OK, I guess, not to be in Heaven; I'm not worthy anyway. OK, here I go, for a second run off the roof. But this time my older brother blocks my route to the sidewalk. I land on the snow pile. I'm still here. God? Are you there? Did you put my brother in my path to stop me from dying? Why bother—I'm not worthy. Father Neary tells me that all the time.

Let me put my head on my pillow and look up at you, nailed to the cross. You were hurt bad, weren't you? You were hurt so bad that you died that day. Can I die today? Please? Let my pain end, too. I hurt really bad too. My pillow is still wet from last night's crying. Let me flip it over and lay my head down again—good, that side is dry from the night before last. I see the sun coming in my window. I feel its warmth. Is that you, trying to ease my pain by warming me with the sun's rays? Can you hear me call to you? I know you went to your Father after your day of suffering on the cross. How much do I have to suffer to have you take me to him too? Yeah, you're probably right: I can never be in Heaven because my soul is damaged by the vile things this man makes me do. He would pray over me afterward, to give me absolution, to help make me into a priest, too. Yes, if I were to become a priest, he tells me I will have to do this to other little boys too. Can this be true, God? Hello? Hello? You must not love me anymore. This has made me so dirty, so vile, that I can't be loved by you. I understand, don't I? If you truly see all and know all, then you know what he did to me, in your name. While placing his private part into my bottom, he made me say your prayer, the Lord's Prayer, along with him. He always repeated "Thy will be done" several times, saying that this is your will. Can it be true, God? I am only ten and very confused. It hurts so bad. This priest says to stop my crying, as my suffering is nothing compared to your suffering and dying on the cross for me. God, you didn't need to die on the cross for me to love you. Do I have to die for you to love me? Maybe if I just dart into traffic, everyone would think it was an accident. Oh, but you would know, wouldn't you? It wouldn't really be an accident; you would know.

Dear God, I pray so much, so hard, to you. Hello? Hello? Maybe I am saying the wrong words? Maybe I am saying the right words but in the wrong order for you to hear? Maybe you don't want to hear me, as I truly am worthless. I am only ten, God. I can only repeat the prayers taught to me. Let me get out my little missal I got for First Communion. How about if I read from that to you? Will you then hear me and help? I can't do this by myself anymore. I can't tell my parents. He said he is connected to you and that he would have my parents taken from me if I told. I don't want my parents taken from me. Remember, I am only ten years old, God. I need my parents. Is this truly your will, as he has told me it is? If it is your will, I am so sorry that I am bothering you. Yes, that must be it; I have angered you, and this is my punishment. I will try to be good; really I will. If I do that, will you then hear me? Hello? Hello? Will you then love me? Can I do anything to make you happy? God, you know I am only ten. Please?

Oh no, he is here again. I hear him talking to my mom. I love my mom. She is a great mom. If this were bad for me, she most surely would not send him upstairs to my room. Footsteps, getting louder and closer—it's him. Can I fit under my bed to hide, and then he will go away? No, I am trapped. I hear the doorknob turn. It is he. All dressed in black, even his jacket, with just that little bit of white near his chin. The collar—your man on Earth. Isn't he your man, God? Hello? Hello?

I see the big grin on his face as I stare up at him. He is so tall, and I am so small. He reaches for me. I begin to shake. He tells me not to make God any angrier with me than he already is with me. God, I do not want to anger you. But is this really what you want of me? It feels so bad, and I have to clean myself up before going downstairs, he tells me. Don't speak a word of this or your parents are dead, he says. He says that he will tell you God, and you will see to it. God, what do I do? Can you hear me? Am I too dirty already for your help?

Soon his arms are around me. It feels like he has ten arms; the more I struggle, the tighter his grip, like a snake, choking the life out of me. OK, he says it's your will. I give in a little, so it doesn't hurt so much. He presses my mouth on his and sticks his tongue into my mouth. What is this? What is he doing? This is your will? Why, God, tell me what I did that was so bad that this is my punishment? I know, I should be better. I should never tease my younger brother. I should do more for my mom and dad and older brother and two older sisters. I promise, God, that I will do better. Please make him stop, please.

As his tongue moves inside my mouth, I feel one of his hands rub me. Rub me in a place that only gets touched to pee or wash when I bathe. What is this? Why is he rubbing me there? He stops. Good. But now he pulls my pants down again. I remember the first time. I had on my favorite blue shirt and my nicely pressed chinos. Mom would always make sure of a nice crease in them. Now they are bunched up around my ankles. He is bending me over my bed. I try to hang onto the bedspread to steady myself. I hear his zipper make noise. I know what's coming next. God, please take me. Take me now. I too want to be with your Father. I promise I will be good in Heaven. Hello? Hello, God? Yes, you are right; I am too damaged to join you. I am sorry, so sorry. Is there any way to please you? Yes. Yes, I'll do what this priest says to do. It hurts so bad. What is he doing? You want me to suffer? I look at the tears dripping off my cheeks as they fall onto the bedspread. Oh no, my mom will think I spilled something on there and be mad. I am sorry, God. I am trying my best not to cry. Will you at least help me to stop crying? This priest is telling me to stop crying, that I am making you mad. Dear God, I am so sorry. I look at his reflection in the mirror near my bed. He is making funny faces. Does it hurt him too? I see your crucifix at the head of my bed. He is right; you had terrible pain. Once again God, I am sorry. Please make this stop. I see him grin and groan as if he is in a really happy state. He is done. Why is he smiling, and I am not? Did I make you madder at me, God? I pray not.

He tells me to stop my crying and clean myself up before coming downstairs. I now know enough to keep a box of Kleenex on the floor under the edge of my bed. Just for his visits. Is he telling me the truth, God? Will you love me if I do what he says? I need your love. I am damaged goods, marked for life by this. He tells me I am special. I am ten years old, and your priest on Earth says that I am special. Once I am ordained, I too will do this to only the special boys. How will I know who is special? God, will you tell me who is special and who is not? Yeah, that's it; you will tell me when I'm older, won't you? OK, I'll stop crying and be better so you will love me. You will love me eventually, won't you God? Hello? Hello?

I stuff tissues in my bottom and make my way to the bathroom. Don't get blood anywhere, he tells me. I know that it has to be private between me and my priest, because I don't want to anger you more, God. As I close the bathroom door, I hear him telling my mother not to worry, as I may be upset. It is very emotional to be "counseled" to become a priest. Counseling? Is this your will, God? I will be good. No, maybe I'll just write another suicide note so my family will know I was too weak to do God's will. They will understand that I was dirty and not good enough for God. Yes, I'll do that as soon as the bleeding stops. Maybe not. Maybe I should try to increase the bleeding somehow until I bleed enough to die. Can that be your will, God?

The upstairs toilet gets plugged often from the massive amount of tissues I flush. My dad is always trying to unplug it. I am ten. Ten years old, God. Will you ever love me? Are you there? Hello? Hello? I come downstairs after I hear him leave. My mom is all smiles; she is getting her family priest. I will dress in black with the white collar, and she will be so very happy. God, this is what you want, right? I forgot to hide the tissue box back under my bed. We don't have much money, and a private box of tissues would not be tolerated. I take some out of each box around the house, small enough to not be missed, but enough to keep a supply under my bed. I must go hide them now, before the box is found. With seven of us under the same roof, no one can have his or her own box of tissues. I did have a whole new box once. It was Christmastime, and I bought one for my grandmother, but I really bought two and hid one for myself.

To this day, at fifty-three years of age, I need close access to tissues. At home, next to my bed, next to my chair, at the table, two in the car just in case I sit in the backseat. Travel? Of course, if there is no tissue box near the side of the bed, I must take the one from the hotel bathroom and put it next to me. It's a quirk that I have. Besides, I never know what nightmares might plague me each and every night. I might need tissues to dry my eyes, or worse, if "he" visits my nightmares. I bolt awake. He was here. I feel the muscles down there pulsing. He's dead, though, isn't he? Or will he always be with me, until the day I die? God, can you hear me? I know he is dead. I saw his obituary two years back, when I was fifty-one. How can he haunt me from the grave? More than forty years has passed. Am I still dirty, stained, and unworthy of your love? I have nightmares, severe nightmares, almost every night. What will stop my pain, God?

Sometimes I bleed so bad that I spend a long time in the bathroom. I feel the pulsing in my hind end. Will it stop? God, can you help me, please? I am sorry for making you this mad at me, but I am only ten, remember. Of course you know—you know all and see all. I remember the teachings. The bleeding is stopping. Thank you, God. I will try to be better so you may begin to love me. Maybe? Hello? Hello?

I sit in the living room with my younger brother. He says, "Hey, Father Neary just turned into our driveway." I glance quickly, and yes, it is his car. Panic—where can I go? Where can I hide to be safe? Nowhere. He is getting out of his car. That all too familiar man of God, dressed in black from head to toe, with that little bit of white collar showing. I run to Mom. "Can I not get counseling today, Mom?" Too late. He is already in the kitchen, big smile, talking to Mom. "Where is Charles?" "Right over there. Come, Charles, it's time for your counseling."

Hasn't it been only yesterday since he was here? Days run together, and I lose track of time. Up the stairs we go. I feel shaky, starting to sweat. We reach the top of the landing, and he takes my arm. We are not even in my room yet. I feel his grip tighten. His tongue darts into my mouth. God, what is this? How will this make me a better priest? It doesn't feel right, but I don't want to anger you, God.

We get into my room. I walk to my bed, trying to brace myself for what comes next. I hear him shut the door, and then he crosses the floor to me. I resign myself to just "stop my whimpering" and offer my suffering up to you, God. We were always taught to offer up our suffering to you, or offer it up to the poor souls suffering in purgatory. I gaze at you on the cross. Yes, this is not as bad as what you must have suffered. OK, let's get this over. If I don't' resist, he will be done sooner.

Not this time. This time, God, he makes me kneel before him and clasp my two little ten-year-old hands together, like when we receive communion. What are we doing? We pray the Lord's Prayer. Your prayer, God. "Thy will be done," Father Neary repeats that part of the prayer. But I am on my knees, staring at his zipper as I look straight ahead. He places his hand on my head and starts to speak in Latin. I know its Latin because we had to learn the Mass in Latin back then. I don't recognize the words, though. Neary says this time it will be something really special, that only very few future priests ever get to do. What is he talking about? What could be that special? Is there something else, more special? At least my pants were still up. I was ruining the crease kneeling, though. I could tell my mom that they were wrinkled from being on my knees in special prayer. That she would understand. It would be OK.

Father Neary separates my hands and places them on his zipper. What is this? What am I going to do? He tells me of Holy Water, that he blesses to become holy. Well, he said, unlike Holy Water, this comes directly from God. It is direct from God, I thought? Maybe this is what I was praying for, to have God love me again. I had been trying extra hard to be good. Maybe I will feel God's love after this. Wouldn't that be great? God would love me. The pain part of my "counseling" is over, maybe. This too, I found out was not true.

As he helped me to lower his zipper, here was this hard penis staring me in the face. It was hard, hairy, and smelly. Why is there hair? I have no hair except on my head. "This is special, just for men of God," Neary said. "You too will be like this when you get older and help other young boys become priests." What was I supposed to be doing? He told me the most special gift from God would soon be coming out of this hard penis. I tried to ask what, but I was told to be quiet and do as I was told. Soon enough, God may start loving me if I obeyed his commands, he told me. He instructed me to cradle his testicles in my cupped hands, just so. Not too loose, not too tight. He would scold me if I wasn't holding them just so. I do not want to anger you, God, so please help do this right. He said to start kissing his penis lightly. All over his penis. He went on to say that something very special was about to happen. Something right from you, God, through him, to me. Neary then told me to begin sucking on his penis, and he began to moan. Once the fluid came from you, God, into him, and then into my mouth, I would be so special. Are you sure, God? This doesn't feel right. I don't like it. He is rocking back and forth. This smells and tastes so bad. Your will, God? Why? This is awful. I wasn't being good enough for you, was I? God, I'll try harder. I will. I really will.

Neary instructs me to make sure that when the fluid from you, God, comes out, that I not spill a drop. I must suck all of it from his penis and not let any of it drip to the floor. This tastes dreadful. It's warm, salty, and icky. Swallow, Charles, swallow. Don't' let any of this drip to the floor. This is the stuff I cleaned off my bottom, isn't it? This is the same stuff that made my hands sticky and awful. God, I am trying my hardest, my little ten-year-old self, to do as I'm told. After I lick him clean, he tells me to go to the bathroom and wash my mouth out with soap, as the final step to please you, God. I did what I was told. I always did what I was told. It is dreadful to put soap in my mouth. God, do you love me yet? I guess not, I feel so dirty, so ashamed. God, what can I do to get you to love me? I just can't go on like this, not any longer. I go to my desk to write yet another suicide note. It's one of countless letters I write and then stare at, only to crumble up and throw into the trash. The trash, that's where I belong. I should be put out to the curb like the rest of the garbage.

God, I try to please you, but I am so bad at it. My mom is Catholic, and all of us kids are too. My dad is Methodist, though, and goes to his own church. Once in a while, my mom lets me go with my dad, as long as it is after going to Mass first, and I cannot pray with Dad when I am there. Are there two of you, God? One for Mom's church and one for Dad's? Aren't you the only God? This is so very hard. Mom makes sure we go to church on all holy days, many times during Lent, and pray the Stations of the Cross too. She makes novenas, and we go to confession each week and then to Mass. We kneel and say our prayers each night before bed. We have fish on Fridays, always. The manger always has a place of honor on the dining room buffet. I stand in front of it and try to speak out loud to you, while being quiet enough to show reverence to you. Dear God, I see you lying in the cradle. Are you OK? If I were there, I would give you my bed. I would sleep on the floor and help protect you as a baby and keep you safe until you were old enough to watch out for yourself. Safe—I want to be safe. I want to feel safe. Until that bright fall day in 1961 when the abuse began, I felt safe. I am safe no more. Where can I find safety? As I sit here, once again I feel the pulsing, the throbbing in my bottom, and it hurts, God. Hello? Hello? Are you there? This is Charles calling to you.

2

CHILDHOOD

My name is Charles Lee Bailey, Jr. I was born in Syracuse, New York, on January 30, 1951, at St. Mary's Hospital in Syracuse, New York. My mother always reminded all of us, including my father, that her faith was number one in her life. She also told me, as a child, that I was "born" Catholic. That was kind of odd—I thought I was born a baby, and I didn't know I was also a Catholic automatically just by being born. To this day, she has said to tell the groups I speak before that I was "born" Catholic.

I didn't realize how that statement would impact the rest of my life and cause her "blind faith" to really make her "blinded by faith" and blind to the horror that would come into my life. I am the fourth of five children, with two older sisters, Carol and "Jane Doe," one older brother, Bill, and one younger brother, Kevin. It's funny, though not ha-ha funny but more like strange funny, that of the five of us, "Jane Doe" (at her insistence to not use her real name) is the only remaining practicing Catholic. She partakes in all the usual things, such as prayer group and missions that meet for about a week, and she is a Eucharistic minister. She would be last on my list to want to be known as "Jane Doe," but I guess she doesn't know what the "do what Jesus would do" saying really means. In the Bible, Matthew tells how Jesus believed that children should be kept safe from harm.

Our family lived in a small gray colonial-style house in Westvale, New York, until I started kindergarten. It seemed like such a good life. Shortly after my youngest brother, Kevin, was born, we moved to Camillus, New York. Both of these areas are suburbs of Syracuse and part of the Syracuse Catholic Diocese. Our Camillus home is a place I would give anything to forget. It remains in my nightmares to this day.

It was a white Cape Cod with black shutters, barely fitting all of us, but it had potential. There was a large yard of almost two acres. We had many enjoyable times in the backyard, playing baseball, football, horseshoes, basketball, kickball—you name it. We all pitched in as best we could to help Mom and Dad remodel our home. My dad knew he could make it nice enough for all seven of us. There were two bedrooms on the main floor and the upstairs was empty and open. All five children slept in one room, while my parents slept in the other. It was like that for a while. I didn't realize then the security I had; if the house had stayed that way, then Neary would never have been able to have access to me the way he did after the upstairs was finished.

In the following photographs, except for the coloring, this is how my childhood home looked when I grew up there. Hidden by the big tree is my upstairs bedroom in the front of the house. My mom and dad still lived there when these pictures were taken. You can see the big back porch roof I jumped off of in the lower picture.

Of course, while remodeling, my parents had no way of knowing that, in the future, the evil man of the cloth would invade their happy home and cause so much pain and suffering to me and later to my whole family. Later, the family members affected by my abuse would also include my wife, my children, and eventually my grandchildren, once they reach the appropriate age to read this book.

I think that people thought of our family like the Walton's on TV. Not wealthy, but having lots of love for one another and trust toward the rest of the world. I remember my mother taking us to church on Sundays without eating breakfast because you had to fast before communion. She would kiss Dad good-bye and hurry out the door with the five of us. Most of the time, Dad would have a hot breakfast ready for us when we returned home. He would crumble bacon on our pancakes as they were cooking, because we never had the money for all seven of us to eat a lot of bacon. That was always all right. We were happy. We were all together for the meal. I did feel very odd that we'd all go to church without my dad. This confused me. Did Dad have another God he prayed to? Were all non-Catholics going to Hell unless we converted them?

I wish that, as a child, I had had a say in what religion I would have liked to be, but in those days my mother thought that she was doing the right thing. She very seldom allowed us to attend the Methodist church my father belonged to and loved. On a few occasions, she would allow me to go with my father, but first she made me go to the Catholic Church for Mass. While devoid of all the ornate statues and expensive trappings of the Catholic Church, I still felt God's presence in my dad's church. These too were people of God, only without the fluff of jewel-encrusted chalices and all the rest. I could not take part in the service or pray at my dad's church, because they were not Catholic prayers. My father and I would come out of the church after the service was over, and he would be beaming from ear to ear. How very proud he was to have any one of us with him to show off to the other members of his church. He always attended church alone, and I could see his sadness about this, even when I was young. He was such a quiet, shy man, but he was also someone who could make you smile by just looking at him. I can't help but think how my life would have changed for the better if only I had had the choice to go to church with my dad every Sunday instead of my mom.

Sue and I were married in my father's church. You could feel how happy he was for Sue and me. His church was a simple brick building with pews and little more. There is no center aisle, but rather a left and right aisle. As you face the altar, Sue and her dad walked down the left aisle. When I first saw her on her dad's arm, it took my breath away. It was like no one else on Earth existed but Sue and I. I remember having to tell myself to breathe. What an amazing moment in my life. It gave me hope. Everyone felt the excitement of our wedding day. My dad got dressed in his tuxedo in a hurry, and he never knew until a visit to the bathroom during the reception that he had not removed his Bermuda shorts before putting his tux on. We all had a good laugh at that one.

I attended Split Rock Elementary School for kindergarten and first grade. I felt like I thought my peers felt. I was a happy little child with a whole world ahead of himself. In second grade at Fairmount Annex, I was still a happy and carefree child. That's where I met "Joe". He was not well liked by my classmates. They would poke fun at him. If he was sent to the blackboard to write, he always returned to his chair with the chalk, which he promptly ate. When the crayons were given out, they were those big fat ones. We would all color, except "Joe", who would eat his box of crayons. When we went for our school physical, all the boys lined up one by one in our underwear. All of us but "Joe", who was naked. He had no underwear. We all stood there in our underwear, and there stood "Joe" naked to the world. Everyone made fun of him except me. I felt so bad for him. I told myself I would be his friend, and I was. I guess that's the type of person I was; I truly believed in being the best I could be, even as a young child.

Third and fourth grade were spent at Holy Family, a Catholic grade school. That's when life began changing for me, although the sexual abuse would not start until I went back to public school. That's not to say that some of the groundwork wasn't being laid out. Looking back, I was mentally and physically abused by one nun in particular. Even at an early age, I was taught to respect and be obedient to adults, so I did what was expected of me without question, like most children. I was a kind, respectful, obedient, and religious child. This made me the perfect target, the perfect mark, for the priest.

One way in which I was different from my classmates was that I was the only left-handed kid in my class. Sister would tell me that using my left hand was the Devil's work and that the demons were in me. She would then beat my left hand with the ruler that she carried. Then she would put my pencil into my right hand and move on, slapping the ruler in the palm of her hand as she walked the classroom. When she would walk away, I would go back to using my left hand. I just could not write well with my right hand. I did not want to disobey her, but I just could not write that way.

Another thing that probably contributed to my later troubles was how we prayed for everyone who was not Catholic. It was like they were some kind of sinners who would never get into Heaven. We prayed for all those who were not Catholic, each and every day, as if they would be going to Hell when they died. I would look at my dad and ask God why he had to go to Hell. He was my dad, and he was a good man. Today I know better, and I know how ridiculous that sounds, but as a child I wondered what would happen to the kindest man I knew—my father. Would he be in Heaven? If not, where would God put that wonderful man who never hurt a fly? And what would happen to my best childhood friend, who was also a Methodist? Would he too not go to Heaven? If I tried to tell my friend about his fate, which was not being accepted into Heaven, he would tell me that I was nuts. I wish now that he would have tried harder to convince me that that was preposterous; he was right, but we were only children. Could Heaven be a place I would want to go if good, honest, moral, loving people were not going there just because they were not Catholic? As an adult, I know better, but as a child, I was confused. One more thought: how could my mom, a devout Catholic, marry a man, have children with him, make sure the children would be raised Catholic, and not his religion, go down that life path, knowing her husband was going to Hell for not being Catholic? That's a big head scratcher to me.

Then, in fifth and sixth grade, I went back to Split Rock Elementary School. And that's when the abuse started. It's rather ironic that I got through Catholic school receiving only verbal and physical abuse, only to be sexually abused by a Catholic priest at release time in public school. I would leave Split Rock and attend release time once a week at St. Michael's. The church was what you might picture in a rural area: a small building that could seat maybe one hundred people. That was where I first met Father Thomas Neary. He was extremely friendly. He had a big smile, and everyone instantly loved him.

He began his path to the prize, the candy, me—yes, me. I was the prize, the candy, his prey. He began by praising me for how well I did in my catechism studies. Then he began to praise me and put his hand on my shoulder. Then he would praise me, put his hand on my shoulders, and walk me out to the bus. Then he added a request to come to my house later to tell my mom how well I was doing. I was so excited; nothing in this world would please my mom more than a priest at our home praising one of her children. How very exciting for her and myself. Little did we all know of the calculated plan he had for me and my whole family. I would never again be as trusting and as innocent as I was before he entered my life. He took my childhood from me and never once looked back—never once considered the pain and suffering he left in his wake.

I will never be able to forgive him, but I'm OK with that because I have been able to forgive myself for being his victim. It is difficult for someone who has never been sexually abused by a priest to understand why a victim needs to forgive himself. The perpetrator makes the victim feel that the abuse is the victim's fault, even if the victim is only ten; it's the victim's fault in the perpetrator's evil mind.

My first memory of something being strange around Father Neary was when he would take other boys behind the altar during release time. He would give all of us a reading assignment and then take one of the boys for some "personal counseling." The boy who got counseling would always come back to class crying. I was never one of those boys, and I don't know for a fact what happened to them, but I sure could give it a good guess today.

Father Neary would instruct all of us to ignore the boys when they returned to class, as they had been bad and were being punished for it. As a child, I just couldn't imagine what they had done to be so upset when they returned. I thought, *how bad could they have been? Should I be scared of Father Neary?* Then I thought, *No, he is a man of God. It has to be their fault, not his.* Little did I know that one day, without notice, Father Neary would show up at my home.

My mom was thrilled that a priest was in our home. Nothing could have made her happier. This priest, this evil being dressed in black with the white collar, told her that I was a boy who would make a wonderful priest, and, with her permission, he would like to start counseling me to become a priest. As I was only ten at the time, it never crossed her mind that anything he said or did would hurt me. In hindsight, Mom's blind faith allowed me to be sacrificed in the name of her religion. He told her that counseling me to become a priest would be so difficult that, almost all the time, I would be sad and crying when he was done and that she should ignore my feelings. He told her that, with time, I would be more accepting to becoming a priest. She never ever asked me what was said in the counseling with Father Neary or what he did; she only continued to be the obedient Catholic. She never saw the pain and the signs that something was so wrong and evil in our home, under the same roof where we all should have felt safe.

She didn't see that I would hide under the back porch if I thought that Father Neary was coming, and how she would have to yell for me because I would hide anywhere if I saw his car drive up. No, she would find me wherever I was, because I would be her priest when I grew up, and all her friends would envy her. How lucky she would be having a priest in the family. It was even better than just being her son—I was becoming a man of God. Her son, what could be better than that?

She didn't see me climb into my closet to make a safe place in my own home. Our Cape Cod home allowed for deep closets. I could get my desk and everything that meant anything to me in there. For the first time in a long time, it made me feel safe. Maybe he would not find me in here.

One thing that my youngest brother, Kevin, told me is that, since we shared that room, he always thought that I didn't like him as he felt I should. I couldn't explain my behavior to him when I couldn't understand it myself. I knew I felt sad and angry that no one in that whole house saw or did anything to stop the abuse. Neary raped me at age ten in my own home with my mom and some of my siblings downstairs. He told my mom not to let anyone up the stairs, and he was stern with his instructions. Neary knew that, by that time, she wouldn't ever ruin the chance of having a priest as a son. Mom would do exactly as she was told and question nothing.

My sister Carol, only a little older than me, would ask why she could not go up the stairs. I wished all the time that my mother would get busy and then one of my siblings would sneak up to save me, or that my mother would bring up laundry to be put away. The "if only" game we all play. If *only*—but what would have happened? That is a question that will never be answered. I'm not sure she could have stood up to her Church. She was a strong woman, but weak when it came to seeing anything wrong in the Church. She believed the three sources of sin were pride, power, and pleasure. Those are things that most healthy individuals strive for, so her beliefs puzzled me. Sue and I have taught our children to take pride in the things they do. Power gives us strength, hopefully to do the right thing; however, this is not always true, as Father Neary used his place of power to commit despicable evil. Pleasure is a big part of our lives. We all get pleasure from our children and grandchildren and pleasure from being intimate with our spouses. I think that my mom really believed that intimacy was sinful, save for bearing children. My mom had even told Sue and me when she overheard us discussing birth control, that why would we need it? Sex was for having children, and we had stopped at the four we wanted. Mom implied that her children were to feel the way she felt.

If my mother had gone to the Church with the allegations of this abuse, I now know what the Catholic Church would have told her. They would have said that Neary was the only one doing that kind of thing, and that they would take care to see that Father Neary got counseling. They would have moved him to another parish. He would have continued his reign of terror on other children. And it did continue, even without the allegations. I am now a fifty-three-year-old man, and Father Neary's youngest victim to date was twenty-six when he told me about his abuse, which started at age six. I believe today that Father Neary was a serial rapist with no reason to stop and no one stopping him.

Father Neary's life of alleged felony crimes extended over forty years. The reason I say alleged felony crimes is because he was never turned over to the authorities. He was at, or visited scores of parishes during his reign of terror, and I have heard of victims from almost all his parishes. The church felt that arranging for counseling and moving him to another parish were enough. He told my mom to pay no attention when he took me up the stairs. Tears would run down my face. I knew after the first rape that something was wrong. It didn't feel holy or right. Father Neary would tell me that God suffered, and who did I think I was? Was I better than God? He knew all the angles, and he used them with the art of a master craftsman. This wasn't some senseless, random act of violence, a one-time occurrence.

In my case; it played out hundreds of times from the autumn of 1961 to the spring of 1963.

I come away with a question. Why didn't someone on Earth, or God himself, help me? So far, no one has quite been able to answer that for me.

3

DINNER IN THE BAILEY HOUSEHOLD

Dinner in the Bailey household was a special time, when all seven of us sat down together around the same table. It was a big, wooden table surrounded by seven mismatched chairs. My dad had remade the kitchen cabinets for my mom. In the kitchen, he had also mounted the biggest homemade chalkboard I had ever seen in a house. It sits in my basement now, and I run my hand along it sometimes, reaching for a happier time. Since I couldn't speak of Neary's doings, in hindsight, maybe I could have detailed it on the family chalkboard? For all to see? It was on the wall next to the telephone. It was about five feet wide and at least three feet tall. It was a note board to all. It was where homework math problems were solved. It was where messages were left if someone was going somewhere. Doctor appointments were listed. It stayed in the house until just a few years ago when the house was sold. On special days, it would be decorated with "Happy Birthday" in colored chalk. Mom always made meat, vegetables, and potatoes. It was a standard. I would sit and listen quietly. My little brother, to my right, shared one end of the table. To my left, sat both of my sisters, and at the far end sat my dad, the mountain in the family. He was slight of build and not very tall, but that was only his outward persona. He towered over all other men, but he didn't know it. At the far right corner near Dad was Mom. She was the glue of the family, the handler of all our day-to-day needs, wearing her apron as she set the bounty before us. Next to my little brother sat the oldest sibling, our big brother. No one ever sat anywhere else except in his or her own chair. I don't remember being told where to sit; it was just a natural thing. It was the way it was, but why? Dinner was a special time to me, when we were all together. I would sit there and soak up what everyone had to say. That is, except when I was teasing my younger brother. It was my duty, you know, to tease him; after all, I was older than he. I did nothing bad, but only what older brothers usually do to younger brothers. As the years passed to adulthood, I regretted how I treated my younger brother. I had to protect him from the evil, from the outside world that I knew about. I could keep him at a distance by teasing. That way, I could hide my pain and maybe save him from it. I would never let Neary take him or be with him. That I knew for sure.

That is the way I was, looking back. My older brother always called me the "Angry American," as I was the first on the scene to aid the underdog. I never hesitated, never. If someone was being picked on at school, I would always get in between the aggressor and his prey. A classmate of mine, who was not allowed physical exertion, was forced to sit out of most activities, as he suffered from heart problems at ten years old. The usual bullies would mock and tease him. Not if I was in earshot, though. I always put myself right between the bullies and their prey. Not that I was fearless, but I never felt fear. I believe I was more interested in helping the others, that I felt needed it, and my own safety and fear never manifested itself. That was one emotion I lacked, somehow. I didn't care how many or how big the bully was. It was going to stop, right there, and right then. I was successful more than not, because bullies are nothing more than cowards with big mouths, especially when around their friends, who were also cowards. Also, I felt if my life went south, maybe, just maybe, my pain would be over. Suicide by proxy maybe? Let the bullies do to me what I couldn't do to myself? I really didn't care about my life all that much and I sensed that the bullies felt it. And today I'm doing the same: getting between the men and women who have been sexually abused by priests or clergy and the big bad bullies of the Catholic Church and their lawyers. I say to them, "Bring it on." I am more than ready for these cowards. I now know, as a fifty-three-year-old man, what is truly right and wrong and exactly "what Jesus would do," as the saying goes—even if others won't, or I should say don't, do what's right.

But I'm getting ahead of myself. Sitting around the table and listening to each member of the family talk of their day, what was new, what was old, and what was the same, I felt safe. No matter what food Mom would serve, I would say nothing, just being grateful for my family. The food served didn't matter, the family togetherness did. It was a happy time for me, and I wanted it to go on forever. Even when there was discord, it was OK, because when dinner was done, we were all there, all family, all still there. Dinnertime was one of the very rare times that I felt genuinely safe.

I had an interest in electronics, in anything electronic that I could get my hands on. Old radios, record players—you name it, I tinkered with it. I once got an old TV from my uncle. It had no case and was dusty, but you could sort of see a picture through the snowy screen. I thought (wrongly, I now know) that if I cleaned it up and dusted it off, that it would make the picture better somehow. I carefully dusted as I watched, ever so eagerly, and I swore the picture was getting better. That is, until I pulled the metal strap away from the picture tube, saw a flash of light, and was hurled across the room. Experience is the best teacher.

I was given a small tape recorder that used those little reel-to-reel tapes about three inches wide. It was about as big as an average-sized book. It had a little microphone attached on a short cord. Before dinner, I would sneak it onto the top of the refrigerator between cereal boxes and let the microphone dangle down the side. No one would see it or notice it at all. As I sat down, I would nonchalantly turn it on. I regularly recorded our dinners. I would wait until dinner was over and then take the recorder from its hiding place when no one was in the kitchen. I would then listen to it through the little earphone that came with it. I did this late at night, when I woke up after the usual nightmare that would rear its ugly head nightly. It was so hard, being ten. I would try to tire myself out so bad that I could sleep, but I didn't want to go to sleep because I knew the next nightmare would be moments away. That is where the tape of the day came into play. Quietly, ever so quietly, because I didn't want to wake my younger brother sleeping only a few feet away in the other bed, I turned it on and listened through the earpiece. Sometimes I would drift off before the end of the tape. Then along came the next round of nightmares. There was a seemingly endless supply of nightmares. All with one common thread, though. They always started and or ended at home. My house, my home. Sometimes I would try to lay awake until morning, thinking if only I could do that, there would be no nightmares. I never made it though; my ten-year-old body would succumb to sleep eventually. I truly believed that some of my nightmares would keep even Stephen King from sleeping.

4

TRIGGERS

Trigger. An unusual word. Literally, on a gun, a trigger is pulled, and the bullet races down the barrel of the gun and on toward its target with lightning speed. That is not all that different from an emotional trigger, except that a person becomes the target, and is not the one activating the trigger.

Victims do not know when something will trigger a response. The trigger could be as broad as a season. One victim I know, a member of my SNAP group, hates the season of fall. He says that he hates the onset of each and every fall. As the leaves change, he feels the tension growing, as his abuse started on an otherwise nice fall day. Another was weeping outside our support group meeting at the library. He was gazing down at a bush, a rare type bush for the area. It was the same bush that was next to the steps to the rectory where his abuse began and continued for years. The unusual leaf, gently moving in the early evening breeze, was enough to send him back as he stood there in pain.

A trigger can be so many different things. It can be a smell, a noise, a taste, or a touch from anyone, even a loved one. It can be a sight or even a shadow that has a certain shape, the sound of a car horn, the pattern on some curtains or a sofa, certain colors and combinations of colors, something physical, an ache or a pain, and a victim is transported back years in an instant. If only we knew how to block out these triggers, then it would be like heaven. They are everyday things we all experience, but to victims, they are triggers.

My wife confesses that from time to time when we passionately kiss and our tongues touch, she inadvertently thinks of the priest who did that to me. It is not on purpose but rather a trigger. The depth of his evil even triggers unwanted, hurtful feelings for a nonvictim. I, too, must confess that, on occasion, kissing triggers the same feeling in me that my wife occasionally feels. That feeling is so disgusting, and we immediately try to erase our minds of it, but not always successfully.

Other triggers are more physical. I had hemorrhoids and had them removed, only to get them back. With hemorrhoids, you have blood in your stool. Even this would trigger me on occasion. I was sometimes instantly transported back forty-plus years ago, sitting there, zoning out, with my mind adrift. Sometimes tears swell up no matter how hard I try not to cry. Thank you, Father Neary.

Music, songs, and lyrics can also be triggers. Rascal Flatts, the country group, had a song out called "Movin' On" that I first heard just before disclosing my abuse to Sue. That song would come on the radio while I was driving, and all of a sudden I would feel tears coming. I didn't know why at the time, but each time the song came on, I would quickly shut off the radio. One time I heard it and forced myself to listen through to the end; I pulled over and wept deeply. To me, that song is one of the most powerful ever written. Now when I hear it, sometimes I weep, but other times it's like a battle cry—I feel empowered by it. I know that sounds nuts, but it's true; I never know how it will affect me.

About the same time, Jo Dee Messina came out with her big hit "Bring on the Rain." This instantly became Sue's battle cry, her empowering song. It says, "Bring it on; I'm not only ready, but I'm able, too." Kind of like "just try to get me, I'm waiting."

Some triggers come out of nowhere and blindside you. My mom, now eighty-six, told me about how Father Neary would come downstairs with his hand out, and she would have money folded up in the palm of her hand. When they shook hands, the transfer of money would happen. He would take it from her palm into his. Each would smile during the exchange. Mom told me this only recently. I cannot understand how Neary could have been so arrogant as to put his hand out for money, minutes after sodomizing me.

What my mother didn't know, or didn't realize at the time, was that she was laying the groundwork for yet another trigger. A few days after telling me this, she came over to have breakfast with Sue and me, as she did most mornings. Sue was at the stove, and Mom sat down across from me. She said hello and extended her hand as if to shake hands with me. This had never happened before. Why would my mom want me to shake her hand? When I extended my hand and took hers, I felt something being placed in my palm. After we shook, I looked and saw that it was money, folded up very small.

I was horrified; I hope I didn't show it, though, because my mother would never hurt me on purpose. It was a fifty; she wanted Sue and me to go to dinner for our anniversary. I placed the folded money in my wallet. I managed to stifle my feelings until Mom left, although it was very hard. Several times while she was there, I felt myself swell up with pain, both physical and emotional; each time, I excused myself to go to the bathroom and hoped she didn't notice. There it was again, the physical pain.

After Mom left, I let out my tears. Sue asked why I was crying. She stopped everything and came to me, holding me, comforting me. "What happened?" she persisted. I told her of the money exchange and what Mom had told me about giving money to Neary.

I told Sue I couldn't touch the money Mom had given me, much less spend it. I opened my wallet and asked Sue to take it out. She could throw it away or do whatever she wanted with it, but I didn't want to see it or touch it. She put it in her purse, out of my sight, and I felt somewhat relieved. I calmed down after a bit and realized that my mom would never hurt me on purpose. Mom loves me. It was Neary I was really angry at, and I wished—as I still do—that he might burn in Hell. In the midst of my tears, I was howling in my mind '*Damn* Neary! *Damn* what he did to me and countless others!'

Here is my anger, many decades after my abuse. I never know when its emotional effects will flare up. Recently, my mother-in-law, Sue, and I went out of town to the wake and funeral of Sue's ninety-two-year-old great-aunt. We knew and loved her. She was a very warm and sensitive woman, and she will be missed. However, during the service at the funeral home, a minister spoke of her passing and how well she was loved by all of us. I have trouble being in the presence of clergy since I disclosed my abuse. The sight of the collar sends chills down my spine. Still, that day, it all went well until the minister decided to close with the Lord's Prayer, the Our Father. Having been abused scores of times while the priest and I recited the Lords' Prayer during the abuse, it strikes a chord in me, deep, very deep because Father Neary would repeat the "thy will be done" verse over and over, telling me this was God's will.

You can't stop a trigger, and you can't avoid it once it starts. Had I known the minister would close by saying the Lord's Prayer, maybe, just maybe, I could have left the room before he started. No such luck. All in unison, everyone started praying. I got up and headed for the door, but by the time I got out of the room, they had already gotten to the "thy will be done" part. Instantly, I was back forty-plus years. As I sat down in the lobby, I felt the all too familiar sickening feeling. It is involuntary; you can't make yourself start or stop the reaction. Years past seem like only seconds ago. You try and tell yourself that it's OK, that he is long dead and can harm no one again. You are OK, try and relax, think of something else. Sadly, it has to run its course and stop on its own—the recovery can't be forced.

As I sat there trying in vain to curtail the mental and physical feelings, I began to feel anger in me swell. How could all these people say that awful prayer? Did they not know? Did my wife say the prayer; did my mother-in-law say it too? My wife, my poor wife and her mom, unfortunately were to get on the receiving end of my anger. The damage these men do is not limited to us; it infects our families and causes pain for them too. I hurried out to the car after Sue gave me my coat off the rack. I was feeling a lack of breathable air in the lobby and wanted out. I got to the car and sat in it. Sue and her mom got in very shortly after me.

I crossed the line then. I asked Sue if she had said the Our Father with the group. She said no, as she had noticed me leaving the room. It wasn't about me, and I had infringed on her great-aunt's funeral. Being as stupid-acting as I was, I continued with something like "you better not have said the Our Father." Stupid idiot, what was I doing? Sue and her mom were mourning their loss, and somehow I had turned it around on me. I committed a major error. They are two of my best supporters, and I had lashed out at them. What was I thinking? Why couldn't I stop going back there? I still felt the pain. From beyond the grave, Father Neary had reached me one more time. Looking back, I told Sue, if only she had simply touched my hand, it would have dissipated the whole thing. Just a simple touch of her hand to mine would have dissolved my hurt. But we didn't arrive at that realization until later, with the help of my doctor. He is truly a master of his skills.

I had hurt the love of my life and her mom. Why couldn't I have stopped myself? Who am I to even ask, much less demand, such a thing as not saying the prayer? I had no right to impose myself in such a way. In a moment, I felt awful, disgusted by myself. I had stepped off the cliff. I needed to apologize to her and ask her to forgive me, but somehow I felt Neary was wringing his hands in delight from Hell.

Perpetrators may physically die, but they can still reach us from the grave. Somehow the evil they commit gets a self-sustaining life of itself. A trigger can come out of the blue, literally. If you have suffered abuse, and you know certain things trigger you, still, you can do your best to avoid them. A case in point, the saying of the "Lord's Prayer," the "Our Father," brings me instantly back to age ten, bent over my bed, being raped by the priest. I do my best to avoid hearing the prayer. Triggers come out of nowhere, sometimes from a stimulus that you didn't know would launch a memory.

My doctor, Dr. Driscoll, and I have walked down many a path of my abuse. Even still, triggers come out of nowhere. They come from places you least expect. Sue and I were cleaning out a closet the other day and came across a box. This box contained my keepsakes. Inside were homemade art from my children's early years. Cards, letters they had written to us and the like. Then, at the bottom of the box was my small black missal from my first communion. Why it was there, I cannot say. How it got in there, I cannot say, or remember, but there it was. The instant I touched it I was back at my childhood bedside, kneeling, praying for God to come help me. I began to cry. What to do with it? I don't know. Why had I kept it in the first place? I don't know. What to do with it now? Throw it out? Sue asked me if that is what I wanted. I didn't want to touch it any longer but could not part with it somehow. It was placed back in the box. Sue felt that maybe this little missal got me through my abuse.

I can clearly remember some of Neary's visits where we are walking up the stairs, hearing the creak of each step, and then I recall the click of the door closing behind him as I walk into my room. Sometimes the last memory is that "click" of the closing door. Our minds are amazing things; they can "shut down" or "turn off" briefly during horrific experiences, and some of those times must be the one where all I remember is that "click."

Sometimes there is an "out-of-nowhere trigger." I was sitting poolside recently, not reading anything, not even thinking anything. I was just sitting there, enjoying the morning sun and its warmth, the special tint of the blue sky, and the big, white, puffy clouds floating by. I had my earphones on, listening to my favorite country tunes, singing along in my head. It was a great morning. Then *bang*! I was back in my bedroom, ten years old once again. What triggered it? A man had walked by the foot of my lounge chair just after getting out of the pool. He was making his way to his towel. I did not see his face, but I could see his torso clearly. He had a relatively flat chest and his nipples were erect, probably from the cool breeze hitting him as he was getting out of the pool. I was instantly, physically sick, and I nearly vomited. I saw his erect nipples, and there I was, back with Neary. I was back in time, sucking on both of Neary's nipples, not too hard, not too soft; I would be scolded until I got it just right, as he held up his shirt. I would follow his directions so as not to anger God any more than he was already mad at me. After all, "thy will be done,"—right???

Watching the eleven o'clock nightly news sometimes sets off triggers too. Sue tries to see if there are clues about what's coming on. Watching yet another young child suffer sexual abuse brings on memories that steal sleep from me or guarantee another nightmare. I like something light before sleep is attempted. Sue and I usually watch *The Tonight Show* for Jay Leno's monologue, and we laugh a little. Most nights, though, I use the relaxation CD that Dr. Driscoll made for me.

5

DISCLOSURE TO MY FAMILY

After holding in my secret for many years, I finally disclosed what happened to me. It was the Memorial Day weekend of 2002, a Friday, at dinnertime, to be exact. Sue and I were up on the shore of Lake Ontario at our camping trailer, where we can sit and gaze out to the west and watch the beautiful sunsets over the water. You can feel closer to God somehow, looking out at his splendor. The gentle breezes, the waves gently lapping on the shore, the fresh air all around, a few birds in flight casting shadows on the water—there is a certain peace up there on the lake, and you are part of it just by being there. There is a certain calmness that's hard to describe. We have had this waterfront campsite for many years now. Our kids grew up there during the summers. Our sons Chas and Jerry were lifeguards there, and later Chas helped develop more camping sites while working for the owner. Our site was the gathering site for many kids—the more the merrier. We all spent countless nights with our children around the campfires. We could look out over the water, see the stars, and see the moonbeams dance along the waves. Jerry and I even saw the Northern Lights once. We would tell each other of our life experiences. The friends of our kids would talk, laugh, and be happy. We would make "some-mores," mountain pies (two slices of bread filled with your favorite filling cooked over the fire in a special cooking iron), toasted marshmallows, and hot dogs. Our site was usually vibrantly alive, but not this night, not this time. This time, just Sue and I were there.

We all hear how God works in mysterious ways, and maybe he does, for this being Memorial Day weekend, it was strange that none of our children or grandchildren were with us. Maybe God knew that that day was the day that Sue would be let into my dark world. That day was the day, and neither Sue nor I knew it.

Once again, another case of clergy sexual abuse of a child was on TV. The Roman Catholic Church sex abuse scandal in Boston had broken early in 2002, and yet another case had been brought forward. The news was doing what it does and what it had been doing seemingly nonstop since January. Another man was telling of his abuse when he was a child and naming the priest who committed the crime. Yes, it was a felony crime, not "inappropriate contact," as the Church would have you believe. I remember one of the reporters saying that a cardinal from Boston had said it was only the priests' way of showing how much they loved the boys—not something terrible. The priests' actions were "misinterpreted" as being something bad. Wow!

Sue was preparing dinner, and the TV was on in the background. I sat with my back to it, as she watched and listened to the details. I looked down and away as I flew back forty-plus years to my own abuse, as I had done numerous times since the Boston scandal broke. It seemed as if that news was on every TV and radio station, along with something about abuse by clergy reported in the papers daily. Sue caught my turning away and looking out the window, and she was annoyed. She thought that maybe I was in sympathy with the accused priests, as I was a product of Catholic upbringing. And so was Sue. She had even attended Catholic grade school.

As for my sympathy with the priests, nothing could have been further from the truth; only my wife didn't know that. She said, "I can't believe yet another boy has come forward. What is wrong with the Church?" She noticed my head turn and drop away. "What's the matter with you? Are you feeling sorry for the priests?" Then she said it: "It's not like you were abused or anything." It was finally too much. The floodgates had opened, and the dam had burst. I broke down in tears as I turned and looked up at her. Sue knew instantly, even without me verbalizing it, that I had been raped by a priest. The shock and horror I witnessed on her face was the most intense look I had ever seen. It took her breath away instantly; she looked like she had just seen the scariest movie scene ever recorded. That image is permanently burned into my brain. She turned off the stove, stopped making dinner, and came to me, arms around me, saying over and over, "Oh, Charley, oh, Charley."

I trembled. I cried. I shook uncontrollably, and the tears streamed from me and onto her as she tried to hold me ever so tight. "It" was out, finally, forty-one years after it was stuffed inward to save myself and others the pain. I had become a master at displaying what was expected of me and not showing how I actually felt. I felt myself melt into Sue's being as she continued to hold me. Safe, I finally felt safe forty-plus years after it happened.

My mind then raced; what had I done? I was not able to come back with a wisecrack or comment to keep it all in check. A sense of horror came over me. *Now that she knows, will she leave me? Will she think I'm some kind of freak, pervert? What? What would she think? How would she act? Was I going to lose her? Stupid, stupid, why was I unable to hold it in no longer? Had I become weak?* If she had asked any other question but the one she did, I probably could have gotten by and kept my secret. My secret, which I had vowed to take to my grave. *What had I done?* Panic, panic was setting in. *How can I do damage control?* My mind raced back and forth—what to say, what to say next to put it back. *Do I tell her all or only answer her questions? Which is it?* I felt myself now sweating, shaking uncontrollably. In the little I had read on the Web sites about victims of priest abuse, their wives had left them, almost without exception. Would Sue be one of the few who stayed, or would she cast me out? *I am so scared, so very scared.*

She wasn't wavering. She wasn't pulling away. She continued to hold me and not let up. Maybe she would stay. *Please, God, make her stay.* She then wept with me. The horror had set in to her too. *Now, what had I done? I had hurt her. What was wrong with me, hurting the woman I dearly loved with all my existence? Stop thinking about yourself, try to "fix" this, and try to stop Sue from being hurt.* It was not to be. Sue was becoming my personal gladiator, even at that moment, and neither she nor I thought it. But, looking back, it started right then, that very moment. I had a partner in this. I was no longer alone in my silent scream.

Was it OK to let go, though? As the days and weeks passed, it became self-evident. Sue was with me for the duration. I saw her hurt turn to anger to rage to yelling out loud, back to hurt and pain. Sue had always told me over the years how she wanted a "purpose" in her life. Not fame, but something to leave the world a little better off than when she came. Sue is an outstanding grandmother, mother, wife, and lover; yes, lover. This, however, was a little more than she planned on. Sue is my number one ally, and she is unwavering in her support. She dares anybody to be mean to me or talk down to me. I am so blessed to have her by my side forever.

Sue's immediate response was to say that we must keep it between us. We must let no one know, no one. As the evening drew on, we wept as I told her the "tip of the iceberg" of my abuse. I feared it too strong to verbalize and too strong for her to endure. Little did I know that she was the rock she is. I was quick to agree with her, to keep it to ourselves. Damage control—on that I was an expert. However, this too came to pass, as early as that night, to an extent.

In giving Sue the sketchy outline of the abuse I was subjected to from the fall of 1961 through the spring of 1963, from age ten to age twelve, I mentioned a call that my mom had made to me only three weeks earlier. My mom had called me just about three weeks before my dam broke, and the only thing she had said, the only tidbit of conversation was "Did Father Neary touch you in any way?" I was mouthing the stern "no" before she even finished her question. And it was over that quick. Later, I found out that she had called me after watching the TV when yet another priest abuse story was on. That was probably one of the shortest phone calls I had ever had with my mom. A simple no and we said our good-byes.

Once I told Sue that only hours after she got it out of me, she said, "We're going to your mother's right now!" And we did. Sue said that Mom must have suspected something because she asked that question. We got to my mom's apartment, and I froze. I could not get out of the car. Sue went in ahead of me to set the stage. She planned to tell Mom that I had something very important to tell her, and it was about Father Neary. My mom was eighty-three at the time, and Sue wanted her to be seated before she came out and got me. *Panic, terror—what was I about to do? I had already hurt my wife, and now I am to hurt my mom?* It had only been a few short hours earlier that I had told Sue.

I felt sweaty, shaky, and tears had begun to form. They had started to slowly run down my cheeks, dripping onto the concrete below me as I neared the door with my head held down. Sue held me as we approached. Once inside, my mom stood. I told her to sit back down. I sat on the sofa; Sue sat to my left, holding on to me; me in the center; my mom to my right. I could see the anxious look on my mom's face. Mom said, "What? What is it you need to tell me?" I said, "Remember a few weeks back when you asked me if Father Neary had touched me, and I immediately said no? Well, he did, for years. Remember the "counseling" sessions to become a priest? Well, he raped me. Where, you ask? In our home, up in my bedroom. Remember how he said we needed to be alone, and we were not to be disturbed? That was why, in my own bedroom. And the car rides for "ice cream"? Never once did he buy me ice cream; he took me to another house and raped me there.

My mom began to weep uncontrollably; I had hurt her as I had hurt the love of my life. What on Earth was I doing? I had spent my entire life putting out fires and performing damage control to everyone I knew, especially my family. Now, what had I done? To my left, my loving wife, Sue, wept, and to my right, my eighty-three-year-old mom wept. I sat in the middle, crying myself. We sat quietly for only moments, but it felt like years; time sort of stood still for then. Sue was hugging me from one side, my mom from the other. We vowed to keep it between just the three of us. No one else need know of this. The three of us agreed, and Sue and I prepared to leave. My mom's parting comment was that she would rather have heard that a family member had died than this. She really thought we were going to tell her of a death. Can you imagine that a relative's death would be better to hear, than to learn of the rape of your son under your roof when you were so close by, just downstairs? Later that same night, my mom called crying and said she had called one of my brothers and one of my sisters and had told them. I felt panic, a gigantic lump in my throat—what had she done? The three of us had less than an hour ago agreed to keep it between the three of us. Mom cried and said she had had to talk to someone and was very sorry. Now what? At that point, I had another brother and sister who didn't know. By the end of that fateful night, the three of us had become five. Mom called many times over the next several weeks, crying and saying how sorry she was, and how could it have happened in her house, under her nose, and she had not seen? Sue and I wondered the same thing. Sometimes the call was just a few seconds long: "I'm sorry, Chuck." She would hang up and walk around her apartment crying. My mom didn't deserve this, and Sue didn't deserve this—why is confession good for the soul, again? What is that about the truth that will set you free? From my vantage point, neither rang true. I saw the hurt spreading through my family like cancer. Killing part of everyone it touches. Changing forever relationships, contacts, and a myriad of other things.

My dad had died a few years earlier. I had never gotten up the courage to tell him before he passed. Neither did I have the guts to tell my father-in-law, who was like a second father to me. Both men loved me deeply, I knew, even though they never mouthed the words.

Telling Sue was something I had tried all our married life, unsuccessfully. We were married thirty years before I told her, which was forty-one years since it had happened. Sue wondered how I could have kept such a thing from her. There were two main reasons: first, I thought she would leave me as others had in the readings I had done. Secondly, I didn't want to hurt her, to see the hurt in her eyes. She was deeply hurt by this, and I felt responsible for it. After all, she was happy before I told her, and it's not like you can reveal something like this, and then it's over, like, oh well, yeah, and it's done. Not with something of this caliber.

It's not like I didn't want to tell her. I did; I truly did. Throughout our marriage, I would practice telling her in front of the bathroom mirror as I combed my hair, or brushed my teeth, or shaved, or just stood there saying it to my reflection. I lost count over the years of how many times I had practiced, but I always chickened out. It was never the "right" time, whatever that meant. Looking back, how can there be a "right" time to tell the love of your life something like this? "Gee, honey, you know, by the way, I was raped by a Catholic priest when I was ten, and it lasted until I was twelve. OK, what's for dinner? Do you want me to grill some burgers for you and the kids? Who wants cheese on theirs?"

Sue was nineteen and I twenty-one when we wed in 1972. At the time, Sue had a little boy who was barely two and a half. I got both a wife and a son. Life was great. We bought our first house and struggled as all couples do, and I couldn't find the right time to tell her. It never felt right. Why would I want to hurt her so? Our son would surely notice that Mommy was sad, and I would have been the one who had made her that way. I must keep my vow of silence 'til death, I thought at the time. Maybe I'd leave a letter for Sue and my children to read after my passing. Wait, that would hurt them too. I had decided that I must keep it to myself and never disclose it. However, as I previously stated, triggers are everywhere. You don't seek them out. They find you. In an instant, I can be right back there, even as I type this. Triggers, triggers.

Sue and I went on to have three more children: a daughter and two more sons. Four kids by Sue's twenty-fifth birthday. Our parents must have thought we were nuts, looking backward now as our adult children wait longer to marry, have fewer kids, and are older than we were when they marry. I wanted eight kids. I always told Sue that. She would say that she had given me four, but the next four would have to be with my next wife. Then we'd laugh. Four teenagers at once tend to keep you busy—so much so that disclosure of my pain was pushed down, deep inside me, replaced by more important things, you know. To break the tension, Sue and I would say, "First one of us to bolt for the door gets the kids. Neither one of us bolted for the door. We also would say ours would be the first case a judge heard where both parents said, "You take the kids." "No, you take the kids." All in jest. We lived for and grew up with our children. Now they are all married, and we have eight grandchildren. Four boys and four girls. Nothing like it anywhere.

From 1972 to 2002, I continued to practice my disclosure in the mirror, and sometimes I would do it out loud when I was alone in the car. That way I could scream, cry, yell, whatever, and be undetected. The conclusion I came to was that there wasn't a "good" time to tell your wife of this. There is no "right" time. Period. So I went on day by day until I finally broke down.

Things that had occurred during our marriage that had confused Sue became very clear after she connected all the dots. After my dad died, I saw to my mom's every need. She had a knee replacement and was in inpatient therapy for a while. The good son I was, I always saw to her needs, but not this time. A little red flag went off in Sue's head how this was different. We saw my mom only once during her rehabilitation stay and then again when she was sent home. Sue knew this was out of character for me; it was behavior like she had never seen before. Sue would suggest that we visit, and I would make an excuse why it wasn't a good time. The piece of the puzzle she didn't know was that Father Neary had been only a couple of rooms down the hall from Mom, at the rehabilitation center recovering from some illness. All I had heard Mom say was his name and down the hall a few doors and stop in and see him. I had hoped Sue didn't see my reaction, and I guess I got it past her. Sue filled in that gap after I told her of the childhood rape. I couldn't tell which room Mom had said or the reason for his illness. All I could do was fantasize about how gravely ill I wished he were. As I said, we never came back to visit, only to pick my mom up. My mom never knew, or did she? It seemed strange that she had never felt bad about Sue and I not visiting, especially since we lived close by, and I have never before not visited mom when she was ill or hospitalized. Sue would pressure me to visit, even if she was unable to come with me. I stood my ground.

I told Mom to call her parish priest, and have him come see her. She did this more than once, but he never came. Weeks passed, still no response. So I called him myself and insisted that he visit her.

About a week after that, he came to see my mom. It was about 11:30 AM, and she and I were on the phone. I said to call me back after he left and let me know how it went. I expected a lot of time to pass before she would call me back; however, it was only 11:55 AM when the phone rang. It was Mom saying that her parish priest had left already. I said, "Mom, what did he say in such a short amount of time?" I thought given her age, and what she had recently been told, he would spend hours there, not minutes. She hesitated before answering me, then said that he was sorry for her pain and that I could see him sometime if I liked. That was all she told me. Two years later, my mom came forth with the rest of what he'd said. He had told her that those things happen all the time, especially in rural areas, and it was common practice for the women on a farm to have sex with all the men in the household, brothers with sisters, all combinations, and it wasn't that harmful. He had told her that people have needs, and these things happen.

I went to see that priest. Sue came with me and, well, I'm sure that nobody else had ever spoken to him as I did that day. Her parish priest had sent my mom a terrible letter about where were her envelopes and money. This letter I brought with me to the meeting. Mom had started spending winters at my brother, Kevin's house to escape the winters here, and the rest of her time was spent at home. Her parish priest's audit of weekly envelopes had showed a gap in Mom's giving. She gave at the church at my brother's home over the winters, thus the gap in her local donations. The tone of the letter is unbelievable, especially for a letter to a woman of this advanced age whose son had been abused. The priest even stated that he knew Mom's problem with the church, but could not take responsibility for it. He made no apology for his letter.

By the end of that night after I told Sue, my mom, my younger brother (Kevin), and one of my older sisters (Carol) had been told. That left my older brother (Bill, yes, his name is really Bill Bailey), the oldest of the siblings, ten years my senior, and my other older sister ("Jane Doe" Bailey, at her request). Mom apologized for telling the ones she did and promised not to tell the others. I said that it was my choice to disclose my story to them and only if I felt it should be. Once again, I was backed into a corner. The disclosure was expanding, taking on a life of its own, so to speak. Could I stem off the rolling freight train? It was gathering speed on its own. At that point, I didn't know it, but, looking backward, I was beginning to take control of my destiny.

My older brother lives thousands of miles away, and my sister "Jane Doe" lives about 150 miles away. I would tell her in person when next we met in a week or so. I called my older brother. Small talk is not my best suit because I stumble, stammer, and sound pretty much like a babbling idiot. What kind of small talk do you make on your way to telling your older brother something like this? "How's the weather in Seattle? Oh, yeah, remember Father Neary? He raped me when I was ten. Still raining, huh? That's what we always hear about Seattle … What? Oh yeah, I did say I was raped at ten. Any sign of the rain stopping?"

My older brother, Bill, always included me as best he could. Even when he went to college and joined a fraternity. Some of the guys would come over and play football in our backyard, and he would include me, even though they would pick me up, ball and all, and carry me for the touchdown. He was always good to me. How would I tell him? How would I start the hurt on him? I didn't want him to hear it secondhand from Mom or thirdhand from Kevin or Carol. There wasn't a good way, so I just told him straight out. "I want you to hear it from me, Bill, not someone else. I was going to keep it a secret for life, but it didn't happen that way." As the story unfolded, I could hear his breathing change, his voice change, and I knew that he was hurting, hurting for me, his little brother. He affectionately calls me "Junior" because I was named after our dad, even though I am fifty-three and he is sixty-three. I could feel my own pulse as I gave him the "tip of the iceberg" and not much in the way of details. We both wept, and then he dropped a bomb on me. He said that one time Father Neary had approached him in our basement while he was playing pool alone and had tried to kiss him. Bill had pushed him off. He had told Mom that Father Neary had made a pass at him and to not let him into the house anymore. Mom dismissed it as Bill just being an angry twenty-something-year-old. Maybe this was the seed in my mom's mind that did not bloom until the Boston scandal broke and she questioned me. I will never know. Bill was mortified, as he asked me where Neary was living then. I told him, "Neary's dead. He died last September." Bill wanted to see me then, but travel money was in short supply.

To make a long story short, the next year I flew out to see Bill for a week. It was comforting to see him again. We see so little of each other. We cried and talked at great lengths, this time with a level of detail that he wanted. He remains my big brother, a special guy in all aspects.

This left my remaining older sister to tell ("Jane Doe" Bailey). She would be in town in a week, and so I waited to tell her in person. She is the devout Catholic in the family, and she is a Eucharistic minister. She runs a weekly mission and holds prayer groups. She is the Catholic's Catholic in every sense of the word. When I first told her, she was mortified, and I sensed a little disbelief on her part. She cried with me after hearing the PG-13 version of what happened, not the R-rated version that my other siblings had heard. She said she would pray for me in her prayer group. Don't get me wrong, I think prayer is good, but I believe that God also wants you to row your boat for shore, not just pray. Isn't it something like this: "God helps he who helps himself?" Pray, by all means pray, but, like I said, still row your boat for shore. What also struck this sibling differently was that Neary had performed her wedding ceremony. Neary left my life after the spring of 1963. A while later, he came back to perform this sister's wedding and was in her wedding pictures. Funny that no one noticed that I was absent from most of the photos he was in, and I pretty much hid most of the day to avoid any contact with him. By this time, I knew that what had happened to me was sex and had nothing to do with becoming a priest. I was sickened, and I feared that if anyone who knew what had really happened to me came out that day, I would somehow be the one at fault. As the day progressed, Neary made eye contact with me and got that grin, that smirk, as he somehow knew that I would not break my silence.

Three of my four siblings said how awful they felt and asked me why I didn't tell them. "Jane Doe," however, said some of those words, but then the next time I saw her was at her son's wedding. After the ceremony and such, we went back to her house. She wanted a few minutes to speak with me alone. OK, we went out to her front porch. No one was there, only us. We sat down, and she said, "Why did you tell me this thing? I don't want to know this."

Does "knock me over with a feather" work here? What an awful, hurtful, and terrible thing to say. "Jane Doe" says that she has no memory of saying that today, but those words burned deep into my brain. I told her that I had wanted her to hear it from me and not from Mom or my other siblings, and how I wanted to be the one who told her, so it would be firsthand. I couldn't believe my ears. Had the most Catholic member of my family just said that she didn't want to know? Man that stung. Just then, we were interrupted by her husband and her brother-in-law, and that was the end of our conversation.

I stewed on it for a while and then had her as a captive audience on a return trip from Buffalo to Syracuse in the car. I had always thought that Neary was an anomaly and not one of scores of priests who did this. I told her of the lies the Church had filled her head with and of the billions, yes, billions, of dollars of wealth the Church owns. The ride was tense for a while. She said, "All you victims want is money. How much is enough anyway? If I gave you a blank check right now, how much would I write it for? A few hundred thousand? A million?" Yet another arrow into my very soul. Every time someone says "how much money," it hurts like a knife clear through me. I asked her, "Who better deserves compensation than a little boy raped for over two years? I can write the one on the check, but there isn't enough space for all the zeros." I went on to say to my sister, "What I want is my day in court. I want to sit before a jury and tell them of a childhood ripped from me at age ten. How I did adult things, perverted adult things, starting at age ten. How I believed that my parents would be killed by God if I spoke a word of it. I want my childhood back. I want to laugh and play, like the other children I used to only watch as a child. My sister remained silent. Then started with the "it was a long time ago speech." In Hosea in the Bible, he speaks of "justice and accountability," and Jesus wants nothing less. Needless to say, the ride was a painful one, and things between my sister and I have remained unresolved.

6

DISCLOSURE TO MY CHILDREN

Then there was the disclosure to my kids. They are hardly kids anymore. They are all adults. The youngest is Jerry, who was twenty-four at that point in time, named after my wife's dad, who was a true monument of a dad in all aspects. Jerry was single then, but is now happily married to Sharon, a wonderful woman, and they have a beautiful daughter. The next oldest is Charles III, who was twenty-six at the time. I got to name him after me. He is now known as Chas, and, at the time, had a son of his own. He and his terrific wife, Stephanie, now also have a daughter. One of each. They say they will most likely stay with two. They are both so adorable. All my grandchildren are. There is something the little ones do to you, and you find yourself talking baby talk to them while you hold them and feed them. I always say that I wish I could somehow bottle that feeling and use it a little at a time on the days that I feel down, as our years grow shorter. The next oldest is our daughter, Tracy, my princess, my only daughter, who was twenty-eight at the time. She had me wrapped around her little finger from the moment I first saw her. And I think she always knew it too. But that's OK; all daughters do that to their dads. She is married to Ty, with three beautiful children—two boys and a princess of her own. The oldest is our son Lee, who was thirty-two at the time. He has a lovely wife, Kathy, and two children, a boy, and a girl. Their son is the little professor of the family, always wanting to learn more, and both are lovable kids. His daughter is never without a smile on her face.

Well, that's the breakdown of my children and grandchildren. How would I tell them? *To tell them or not to tell them? That is the question. Maybe they should never know? Do they need to know? Will it hurt them as it did my wife, mom, and mother-in-law? After all, I am the protector; I tell them all, "I am the man of steel." No harm can come their way. Will they think I am weak? Will they think I am dirty? Will they be disgusted by me? Will they be repulsed? I am sweating, shaking, and won-*

dering if this is the right thing to do? Yes. No. Yes. No. Yes. Sue assured me that all would be OK, that I was underestimating our children. Sue told me to give them more credit. *But I am damaged goods. I am surprised that she has stuck with me all these years. Is it out of pity that she stays with me? How am I worthy of her love—or that of my children?*

I ran through my head all the possible scenarios I can think of. None, not a one, seemed to fit. Maybe I should have stood my ground and said no more. No more people needed to know. *How can it possibly be good to tell them of my pain? Will they cry? Will they never look me in the eyes again, only talking to me with their heads turned away in disgust? How can I ask them to understand, when I am the one who suffered this pain, and I don't understand it myself? I love my kids so much. Must I once again be the protector of all? The "man of steel" is beginning to rust, and no one must know!*

I swore Sue to secrecy, to vow not to tell anyone else. After all, that was what she first thought we should do. Tell no one. I was a little intimidated, though. I had testified before the New York State Senate hearing about my abuse and about changing the law to protect all children and then found out the very next morning that the newspaper had put out an article about my Senate hearing speech, naming me by name, but not my predator; he was only mentioned as the "alleged abusive priest." That sounds fair, right? Put the victim's name out there, not the evil one's name. It was done, it was out there, and there was nothing I could do about it. Then the TV news channels came to interview me. It's out there, for sure. Well, if I can no longer keep a lid on it, then here I come. Proactive—that is the path I would then take. Like it or not. You want the truth? Maybe you can't handle the truth.

Two of our adult children live out of town, two close by. Sue thought I should tell Jerry first. No matter what anyone says, there exists part of a parent that keeps each of his or her adult children as a child, in some small way. You are a parent for life, like it or not. A part of you "parents" your adult children, no matter what age they are. Telling my children will be hard, very hard.

Unknown to me, Sue had already tipped her hand to Jerry and told him what I wanted to talk to him about. Telling my wife was tough enough, let alone telling our kids. My mind raced from one end of the spectrum to the other. *What if Jerry is repulsed by me? What if he thinks less of me? What if he forever sees me as weak and damaged? Tell him. No, don't tell him. Yes, tell him. No, are you nuts? You can't tell him what happened to you as a child. OK, tell him. He will understand. No, don't. He can't possibly love me after he hears what this priest did to me. I am not giv-*

ing Jerry enough credit. While he is the youngest of four, he is deep and silent, not unlike me.

Can I win this wrestling match? Maybe tomorrow, or the next day I will tell him. I am getting sweaty, shaky. Does Jerry see this? Can he sense it as I do? Will he forever think less of me? I must tell him. But when is the right time? Is there ever a "right" time? Ever?

I looked at Jerry as he sat only a few feet away. Sue got up and went to bed to leave us alone to talk. Jerry watched Jay Leno and his monologue. This was a bad time. I told myself to buck up, be a man, don't shy away from it. My mind raced with all the bad things he could think of me after telling him. Our father-son relationship would forever be different. Different bad?

Sue came back into the room and turned off the TV, turned to Jerry, and said, "Dad needs to talk to you." That was it; the cat was out of the bag. I felt consumed with fear. *Have I just fallen off a cliff? Can Jerry sense my panic?* I felt tears coming, and I hadn't said word one. *I must pull myself together. I can't fall apart. I am the Dad, the Father, and the "Man of Steel." I can't expose my weakness, or can I?*

As a parent, I give all my children unconditional love. They may do things as adults that I may not agree with, but that is part of raising them and setting them free. My love is forever and boundless to my kids, and they must know that. Don't they? I know I loved my dad without reservation until the day he died. I know my mom loves me too; she, at eighty-six, still tells me that she loves me. After all, Sue still loves me, and she knows all the gory details. There I go again: the trust issue seems to come out a lot. I find it so hard to trust because I was betrayed by that "man of God," that "Holy Roman Catholic Priest," that representative of God on Earth.

I thought, *this is my son, so I can trust him. He loves me. I know he does.* He is as shy and quiet as I was until that fall day in 1961.

I began, I said, "Jerry, I have something to tell you. I don't know an easy way to start. I search for words to express to you how I feel and what happened to me as a child. There is no sugarcoated way to say what I am going to tell you. I love you dearly. You have been a great son and have grown to an adult I am so proud of." I went on to say, "Your grandfather, my dad, would be calm in the face of anything that crossed his path. I always joked to you kids that even if our house were on fire, my dad would probably simply say, 'Our house is on fire, and we should probably go outside.' My own dad was a man among men for sure."

"Jerry," I began again, "what I have to tell you is probably something you would never expect to hear from me. As a young boy, age ten, I was raped by a priest. I use the term raped as opposed to any other term you have heard or seen on TV or in the paper because that is what it was. It was not 'inappropriate contact' or 'a mistake' as they like to call it. I am not a mistake. A priest had anal intercourse with me from the fall of 1961 through the spring of 1963, from age ten to twelve." I see the tears coming from Jerry's eyes, as he tries to hold them back. *What have I done? What have I done? I have hurt Jerry; I have hurt him beyond repair. That bastard brought me to this point. It's not bad enough that the love of my life, Sue, was forever hurt by my telling her, and I see the hurt my mom suffers too, but I now have hurt my son, my youngest child, Jerry. What is wrong with me? I knew I should have kept it to myself. I feel like I am spreading a "cancer" to my family. How can any good come from this? I take people who mean the world to me, and then I hurt them, one by one.*

Jerry could no longer hold back the tears as I tried to apologize to him for telling him of this evil from my past. I looked into his eyes, now a flood with tears—tears I caused. Tears that would not be if I had not told him of this horror. *Have I ruined my relationship with Jerry? Will he ever be able to look me in the eye again? Will his love for me waver and leave? Damn that priest, damn me for not keeping my secret until I die. Jerry is hurt and I did it to him.*

After telling him a shortened version, with as little detail as I could, Jerry asked me one question. "Dad, where is he?" This response was not what I expected. Jerry, as I said, was the calmest of all of our four children and not the one I thought would want to know where this priest was. I told him that Father Neary had died in September of 2001; at the time I told him, it was the summer of 2002. I sensed a feeling of disappointment in Jerry's voice. He was twenty-four years old at the time and would risk the rest of his young life to settle a score with this worthless piece of human waste, because he loved me that much. Yes, he loved me that much. It made me cry even more at the return of unconditional love from my son. He now knew of my past, and he still loved me. I wept deeply for several moments, and Jerry came over to me and put his arms around me, telling me it was OK, he loved me, and it would be OK. Had we just switched roles and now I was the son and he the father? He was concerned only of my well-being and his love for me, nothing more. I was humbled by this. I felt like I have never felt before. Jerry loved me still. He really did.

After Jerry knew that the bastard was dead, I sensed that he felt a little cheated by that fact. Then, Jerry told me his analogy of me. Jerry said, "If all the dads in the world were precious gems, you would be the diamond." He had said so much, in so few words. What a loving son I have. My wife still loved me, my mom still loved me, and my son still loved me. How could this be? I still viewed myself as dirty and damaged goods, not worthy of anyone's love, but I had their love. I felt that I would be OK, maybe. I still had three other children and their spouses to tell. How would they take it? Should they know, or should I stop telling people?

I thought, *if I stop here, the remaining children might see me on the TV news or in the local newspaper. Since my hand was forced when the paper ran my story, it was out. No going back now.*

Chas, as he likes to be called—he is Charles III, as I am Charles, Jr.—selected his nickname as a teenager. Stephanie and Chas have a son. Gotta love it. He is nicknamed "little man." I am blessed to have them. My dad would have really liked to live long enough to meet these great-grandchildren.

I decided that I would tell Chas alone. I wanted him to make the choice to tell Stephanie or not. I had a deep fear that my daughters-in-law and son-in-law would ban me from seeing my grandchildren once they knew what had happened to me. I would lay down my life for any one of them, even if rejected by them. I would hate it to hear that they could not trust Grandpa alone with the grandkids. I would be victimized all over again by that. I have to admit, though, that their concern follows the media. We have all seen, read, or heard of some evil person doing evil to a youngster, and then they say, "Well, it happened to me as a child, and that's why I did it." And sadly, they sometimes get absolution from the public at large because supposedly they couldn't help themselves. To that, I say an empathic *no*. *No way, no how!* Life is choices. Choices every day. Each day we get up, we choose our daily path. We are not led around on a leash, responding to another's tug or pull. Each day, we choose what we say and what we do. Choices, all choices. An abuser chooses to commit evil on a child. It can't be blamed on the fact that "it happened to them." Stop right there. When caught, what do they say? Usually something like this: "I was wrong I know it was bad, but I couldn't help myself. It happened to me as a child too." Politely put, *bullshit!* Do not give these people sympathy or empathy. They are evil, truly evil, as anyone who has been on the receiving end of their attacks would tell you. We all have urges, but we all don't act on them. We choose not to, and it's a conscious choice: don't do it.

How would I tell Chas? How would he take it? He is a big guy. He has been weight training since seventh grade, and he played Ironman football in high school and then college football. You would not want to be on the receiving end of a tackle by this guy. He would not stand for anyone harming his family. I knew he loved me deeply, and would most likely be hurt by my telling him, just as Jerry had been. I must admit that I had always felt that if I ever disclosed what had happened to me, it would be on my terms and at my decided pace. Not happening. I needed for my family to hear it from me and not via the media.

Chas and I sat quietly. I stuttered and stammered, like a little kid. Off to a bad start. Doing the right thing is the hardest thing anyone can do. I began to tell him of Father Neary and what he did to me as a young boy. I could see two things happening: one, he was beginning to tear up, and secondly, he was tensing his muscles hard. I only gave the same sketchy details that I had told Jerry. The gross details I kept to myself. I could see the hurt in Chas's eyes from what I had told him of my abuse. It was awful to think that telling the truth could hurt so much. Chas, like Jerry, hugged me and, for that brief moment, I was the child and he was the dad. They both wanted to help and protect me. I can't find the words to accurately describe how I felt and how they reacted. How had I become the child for that brief embrace? Sue and I have raised two amazing men. Then Chas, like his brother, said, "Where is he?" "Thankfully, he is dead," I tell him. "He died over a year ago." It is lucky for him that he's already dead, as Chas would have snapped him like a twig, without any hesitation. Chas would fiercely defend any family member. I remember Chas one summer, coming to the aid of his younger brother who was on his way to get ambushed by some kids. Chas put a stop to it before it started. On the walk back home, Chas said that only he could pick on his brother, and no one else could!

I went on to tell Chas of my fears that Stephanie would no longer want me around her or around "little man." I told him how that would hurt me so much, and that I would never harm my grandson or anyone else. Chas stopped me there. He said to stop. He already knew that. I didn't have to say it. I left it up to him to tell or not tell Stephanie. He asked if I was sure Neary was dead, and I told him yes. I don't think he believed me.

A few days passed, and Sue and I stopped by Chas and Stephanie's to see them and little man. Chas greeted us and hugged and kissed us as he always did. I then looked down at little man running toward us, hugging our legs. I looked up to see Stephanie walking toward me. I saw tears running down her cheeks. Chas has told her. She hugged me, and we both cried. Stephanie apologized for what happened to me, as if it were her doing somehow. She too was hurt, deeply hurt, but still she loved me, even knowing what she now did. She held me tightly, and I told her of my fears that little man would not be able to be with Grandpa anymore. She put my fears to rest without a second's hesitation. She too asked where Neary was. Was he truly dead, as I had told Chas? Stephanie imagined out loud how awful it must have been, as we wiped our tears from our faces. I was amazed that I was still loved, even though I am damaged goods; I am working on that.

The two remaining children lived out of town. Our oldest son, Lee, lived in Milford, Massachusetts, a suburb of Boston, at the time. Our daughter, Tracy, lived in Fuquay-Varina, a suburb of Raleigh, North Carolina. Sue hinted to Tracy on the phone that we would be seeing her soon, and that we had something to tell her. Sue's hints gave Tracy an idea of what was to come.

We traveled to Lee's home on our way back from a trip to Stowe, Vermont. My mother-in-law owns a week's time-share there at the Trapp Family Lodge. We arrived at Lee's and were greeted by his wife, Kathy, our grandson, and our granddaughter. It was good to see them. Later that night, when the kids were in bed, and even Kathy had retired for the evening, I tried to tell Lee, but just couldn't. I feared his response. I went to bed, and Sue sat up with Lee to the wee hours of the morning. Sue told him of my abuse. He was visibly hurt. His first reaction was to want to tell no one, not even his wife. It was after 4:00 AM when Sue finally came to bed. Lee and Sue had talked on several topics and not just my abuse. Sue told me of his wish to tell no one, not his wife, Kathy, or his in-laws, who lived only a few miles from our home. His in-laws already knew, if they had watched the local news or read our only in-town paper. Lee's in-laws are the strictest of Catholics.

Morning came, and we were awakened by our grandson and his smiles. It was breakfast time. As I ascended the stairs, I began to feel weak in the knees. How would Lee greet me? Would he say anything? Would he hug me? Would he hate me? Would he say that I should have kept quiet about this? The first adult I saw as I walked into the kitchen was my daughter-in-law, Kathy. She came to me with teary eyes and hugged me, saying how sorry she was that I had to endure the abuse. So, I guessed that Lee had decided to tell her, after all. Lee entered moments later and he too hugged me and said he was sorry, as if he had had any control over it. They both said that there was no fear of the kids being with Grandpa. I left the room to cry in private, in the bathroom. I was relieved and hurt once again, as I had spread my hurt to more of my loved ones, only to be embraced by them too. How could any of them love a person as damaged as I? I still felt dirty, ashamed, and embarrassed, but I am working on it.

The last to tell was our daughter, Tracy, my princess. She is a strong, brave, young woman. A good mix of both my temperament and Sue's. She is married to Ty, and they have three children, two boys and one girl. Soon after Tracy arrived from out of town, to our camping trailer, Sue took the kids for a walk while I sat with Tracy on the big wooden yard swing that our children bought for us for our twenty-fifth anniversary. There was something about the gentle motion of the swing, the evening breeze coming off the lake, as I felt the fading warmth and the setting of the sun. I told Tracy my "secret." Tracy had prepared herself for this, as she thought that something had happened to either me or her mom. We talked, cried, and hugged. I spared her the details of the abuse. Tracy, too, said she was sorry. I guess that is hard because the ones who should apologize don't. While Tracy's husband, Ty, was not present when I spoke with Tracy, he had also asked where he could find Neary. Just like Jerry and Chas had done.

I had underestimated my family. My wife, kids, and their spouses all still love me and want me in their lives. Our daughter says we can have the grandkids even more often if we wish.

What was I scared of? How could I not trust my family? Ah … there it is one more time, that word "trust." A word I will wrestle with for the rest of my days.

7

SAFE

Safe. Such a small word. Safe. Just by saying it, you can feel its meaning. Safe. A four-letter word. Many words have more letters and more syllables. It is a very small word, but read on, and you'll see why it is a word with the utmost importance, especially in a child's world.

We use the word safe when we talk about protecting things like our "stuff" and our money. We take things to the bank and store them in a safe. However, even that is not "safe" enough for us. We then rent a special box, a "safety" box, inside the safe. We treasure our things so much; too bad we don't always treasure our children. Money, jewelry, and stocks are all safe in our safety deposit boxes inside the big safe.

We use the word "safe" in sports. An umpire decides if you're safe, on first base, on second base, third base, and finally home. Safe at home. Safe at home—that's what our children should be, without any compromise. Above all of our things, children should be safe. They should have the safest surroundings at home. Sadly, that is not the case when it comes to some sexual abuse cases by a Roman Catholic Priest. We can't be with our children all the time. Sometimes they are away from home; however, at home is where they should feel safe from the "outside" world and all its pains. When a child has had a bad day outside his or her home, then that child deserves nothing less than to be safe at home. That should be true without exception.

Personally, when I say "safe," it brings up the idea of being warm, comfortable, secure, and protected from harm, as if there is an invisible barrier surrounding me. I was safe at one time. I felt safe until that sunny fall day in 1961 when the abuse began, at age ten. After that, my "safe at home" was gone. Little did I know how much those experiences would haunt me the way they do today. Anger, boy, do I feel anger, frustration, and rage almost like I am standing naked in a crowd and screaming, "Don't you see me? I am here. I have been violated in the most heinous of ways by a 'man of the cloth,' a priest. God's representative on Earth. Who can I turn to? My mom and dad will be taken from me if I tell."

This must be what they mean by "suffer in silence." My childhood stopped, like a freight train running off a cliff. It is strange; you can actually feel your sense of "safe" stopping in an instant. Not over time, but in an instant. Ten years old—what to do? What to do?

I remember nightfall on that first night. My younger brother and I climb up the stairs toward our bedroom with the same cadence as the priest had used. I am in front, and my younger brother is behind me. Step, step. I could feel my pulse, my little ten-year-old heart, pounding, pounding in my little chest. I should have let my brother go first, not me. He climbs into his bed. I stand and stare at my bed. I look up at the crucifix over my bed, and glance at the mirror. Is that his shadow on the wall? It can't be; it's just my brother and me in the room. Shadows, only shadows. But now they bother me. I'm sure they were there last night, but tonight they frighten me.

I glance over at my brother. He is already under the covers, eyes closed, and facing my way. He is safe. He feels what I felt last night but will never feel again. That tiny four letter word: safe. He looks like he hasn't a care in the world. Once the line of safety is crossed, it is a one-way street, with no turns and no "take backs." The safety is gone. It's the glass of milk you spill and watch as it spreads over the table, spilling onto the floor. It's out of control, and you can't stop it or change it. All you can do is try to contain it so it doesn't spread to others. I can't ever let my little brother feel unsafe, at least when he's at home. This became my mission, although I didn't even realize it until I reflected backward, over the years.

I pull back my covers, crawl into bed. What is that? Is he here? No, just another shadow, cast by the headlights of a passing car. My light on the nightstand is still on. I turn it off. Darkness. I feel tense; I feel my bottom throbbing still. I must get up and check it. How could I explain blood on my sheets to my mom?

I was right. I was bleeding again. I sit there praying, as I did many times after this. *Stop, please make it stop.* I return to my bed. Under the covers, I sweat, and I feel awful. Do I dare close my eyes? What if he comes back? "Safe at home"—never again.

I go to school the next day. It hurts to sit on the old wooden chair at my desk. His memory flashes over me like I am being hit by a brick. Surely he is not here, and my classmates are around me. I am not alone, and today isn't release-time day. Today we will not be going to that church where he is.

Many fitful, sleepless nights followed. He came again for other "counseling" sessions. Over time, I learned to make my mind drift, consciously taking myself to another place, another time, anywhere but there. No longer did I resist, because it was useless; he was too big. It always hurt more when I fought it. And the more I fought it, the more I was told that I was angering God. I somehow got to a point where I was just there physically, but my mind was elsewhere. The one and only thing I could control was my mind. *Let him do his thing and leave me alone!*

I felt scared to come home because his car might be waiting there for me, or he would already be in the kitchen with my mom, waiting for me. I guess I became his "afternoon snack." *Rape the little ten-year-old. No one sees him. No one hears him. He is invisible. He is disposable. He is not worth loving.*

Every house has creaks, noises, and the like. As I lay in bed at night, the noises all became him. *I just know he is coming. I just heard a footstep. What was that noise?* I lay there, weeping. I feel the cool night breeze come over me. It makes my tears feel even warmer as they slowly drip from my eyes. *I must be quiet. I cannot wake my younger brother. He will ask questions, or even worse, he may summon Mom. How could I explain that?*

Safe—I want to be safe. How can I do it? Is there somewhere I could go? Would I feel safe there? I have nowhere to go.

Our bedroom had really deep closets, as it was upstairs in a Cape Cod style home. There were two closet rails, one high, and one low. With the clothes spaced just right, there was an empty space back there, behind the clothes where no one could see me when I hid. If someone opened the closet door, I was out of sight, and if I held my breath, no one would know I was there.

Safe—how I wanted to feel safe again. I moved my little desk and lamp back there, facing out, so I could have my back to the back wall of the closet. I brought some of my favorite toys to play with too. I was *safe*. At least I thought I was. My younger brother thought I was weird. That was OK. I didn't have to explain to him what I was doing. Most of my free time at home, I was back there. It was a small, cramped place, but it was safe. No, I still didn't really feel safe, but it was the best I could do. I would sit there reliving his visits from time to time. The memories would creep up on me, and I never knew why. What would trigger it? A passing car? Someone calling me? Many a time, I would sit there, writing my suicide note, over and over, and each time I would end up crumbling it up in anger and tossing it away. *Kill myself? Why not? What was left for me anyway? God didn't love me. Father Neary had told me so.* My mom could not hear my silent screams.

Suicide? Why not murder suicide? That's it. Kill him and then myself. Why not? How could I do it? After all, if I killed a man of God, I would surely be going to Hell anyway. Maybe on one of our drives? I could grab the steering wheel and run us into a tree. Or sneak a big knife from the kitchen and hide it under my mattress. Then, just as he was "counseling" me, I could turn around and kill him and then fall on the knife myself.

Yet another night like the previous one. Lying in bed crying and plotting. Another gaze toward my younger brother. Such a peaceful look on his face. He sleeps soundly, and he feels safe. "Home safe."

I began to create a world in my head. *I will be powerful. I will be strong. I will be safe.*

One time, I put a string, a fine thread, tied to each side of my bedroom door. You couldn't see it. It was about knee-high. My brother knew it was there, and we carefully stepped over it when we left or entered our room. If you walked in and broke the thread, a car horn in my closet would go off. I hooked it up to a battery in the closet. One afternoon, as I was in the backyard, I heard it go off. Who was it? Turned out it was my mom, and she didn't much care for it. That was that. I wanted "him" to trip it, not my mom. I then took my little battery-operated tape recorder and hooked it up to work as a mike outside my room so you could announce who you were before coming in. That too failed, as there were no locks on our bedroom doors. Another failed attempt to create a sense of safety.

I spent countless hours in back of that closet. I became anyone I wanted to be. I was a judge, sitting at my desk, and all who passed before me were guilty as charged. No one in our family of seven ever noticed or said anything to me about my time there.

There was one place that did give me a sense of safety. It was our tree fort. Dad and my older brother had built it way up high in the sky. It felt like an impenetrable fortress. As I got older, I noticed it was but maybe ten feet off the ground, but as a little boy, it felt like a mountaintop. From time to time, we were even allowed to sleep in there. Once in the fort, we pulled up the ladder through the trapdoor, and no one could reach us. No one. A small, safe spot. We would play Cowboys and Indians up there. We were sometimes the cowboys, but sometimes the Indians. We would pretend to shoot the bad guys from the safety of our fort. However, I was shooting "him" a lot of the time—not cowboys or Indians. My little brother didn't know.

Safe. The biggest little word in our language.

8

RAPING MY INNOCENCE FROM ME

As I write this, I find myself drifting between being the fifty-three-year-old and the ten-year-old little boy whose youth, innocence, and love of life were ripped from him. The boy keeps looking for help. Any help. An exit to leave—maybe even an exit from this Earth. The boy sits on the back porch on a nice sunny day in early fall. Just right. I hear a car come up the stone driveway. It can't be my dad, as it's too early for him to come home. It's him, I can just feel it. I usually know when his visits are scheduled. Maybe, just maybe, I can make it to my safe place. I glance down the long stone driveway. It is him. The screen door slams behind me. Mom knows I am on the back porch, and I'm sure she probably heard the door slam as I scurried out into the big backyard. I round the back of the garage, climb the chimney, crouch down, and hide. I am safe. No, Mom is calling me, and she knows I am not far. I hear her voice getting louder, calling me as she draws nearer. She knows about my safe place. Oh no!

I climb down and tell her that I don't want to go with Father Neary in his car. I know what my mom must not know. A trip in the car means only one thing. I must tell her today, but I can't risk God taking her from me. Surely, if she knew what lay ahead she would not let me go. My mom loves me. She hugs and kisses me. Kisses not like those of Neary. No tongue in my mouth. No smell of the pipe he smokes all the time. As we near the driveway, I can smell the scent of his pipe before I see him standing by his car. The usual big grin on his face. As we get near, he comes toward me. I can feel the sickness growing in my stomach. I know what's coming. God, is this truly your plan? Are we going today in his car and hitting a tree, so we both die? If it ends my pain, it's OK. After all, Father Neary says you love me only when I please him. I am going to be a priest one of these days. Father Neary will tell me when it is to be. Dear God, this is so hard for me to understand. He tells me I will know when it is time. Yes, I will offer my suffering up to you, as I have been told many times. Offer your pain up to the Lord. Since I am not being crucified on the cross like you were, my punishment must be this, to go with Father Neary.

Wait, I know how to use tools and work with wood. Maybe I can build my own cross up in the woods behind my house. It is very dense with trees and shrubs. I could build it out of sight, and no one would find me before I came to you. Yes, that's a great idea. Then my suffering would be like yours, and then I would come home to you as you did to your Father. No, God, I guess you're right. Even if I could build it in the woods behind the house and I dug the hole for the cross, how would I be able to drive nails into both my hands? I could do my feet OK and one hand, but without both hands, it wouldn't be good enough for you, would it? Once again, I would fail. I am so sorry that I am not worthy of your love.

In an instant, panic, I check my pockets. Every time I go in his car, I am to have toilet paper in my left front pocket and tissues in my right front pocket. I frantically check, first my left front pocket, nothing, then my right front pocket, nothing—nothing in either pocket. What do I do? Father Neary will be mad, and you will be mad because I am not doing what he wants. Quickly, I tell my mom I need to go to the bathroom. I didn't really have to go, but I could stuff my pockets with the needed toilet paper and tissues. I hear my mom call to me to not keep Father Neary waiting. As I get into Father Neary's car, and the door shuts, I know what is coming. I feel myself shaking. Mom, can you not see how much I don't want to go? His counseling sessions to make me into the priest you want, sicken me. Look into my face, my eyes; can't you see the pain I feel? As we pull out of the driveway, he has me slide over next to him. So he can hear me better. But I know the real reason why. I have taken this car ride before. It used to be I sat on the passenger side and that was OK, but then he made me sit closer. He couldn't hear me as well with the noise the wind made from the open window.

The first ride I went on, we just rode around as he spoke to me. I sat in the passenger side, as anyone would. He gave me instructions on what to wear and the necessary toilet paper and tissues to have with me. I don't know why each had a specific pocket, but I didn't dare get it wrong or ask about it. That's why this visit I wasn't prepared. I did not know he was coming. As we drive away, I slide over next to him. Barely out of sight of my home, I feel his arm around me pulling me ever so closer. I look at the statue on his dash and tell myself that this is what God wants. Now I am tight next to him. We slow to a stop at the stoplight. He turns and thrusts his tongue into my little mouth. I cannot escape because he is so big and I am so little. He is in his usual priestly dress, with that little bit of white showing. My eyes dart around; can't any of the other cars see this? Can they not see me struggle? It feels like I am making eye contact with someone, only to have them look away as soon as our eyes lock.

By now I know the route to where we are headed. As we pull into the driveway, he lessens his grip on me. We go up the stairs and into this house. It is full of very old furniture, like my grandma's house. A woman is there with a plate of cookies. Who is she? His mom? His friend? His sister? I never get introduced. She must have known that we were coming, as there is also a glass of milk already set out for me. They talk quietly to each other as I eat the cookies and drink the milk. Then, Father Neary leads me to a back bedroom and closes the door. I know what's next. I begin to cry. Neary says not to anger God anymore than I already have. I try to fight back the tears. I offer my suffering to you, God. Please help me through this. After he finishes, I use the prepared toilet paper and tissues. He said it would be rude to use the toilet paper and tissues in this bathroom because it was not my bathroom. As I head for the bathroom, I hear him making conversation down the hall with the woman. He was in a hurry today and was not the least bit gentle. I hurt, really hurt bad this time. Although we did pray briefly after the rape, and he finished in Latin, saying something only you and he would know, God. Maybe you would now start to love me, God?

God, I don't feel your presence, only the physical pain. I make sure the toilet paper flushed and the tissues went into the trash can. But how, so no one would know? The solution came easier than I thought. There were newspapers in the bathroom at home and some wadded up into balls in the trash can. I opened one a little and saw a bloody bandage inside. So, others in my family are bleeding too. I felt a little better knowing I was not alone, but where were these bandages? I can't ask because Father Neary said I could not say a word to anyone. OK, maybe later he will give me bandages too. Are others in my family being counseled too? Not by Father Neary, though, because I was the only one he saw when he came over and the only one to leave in his car. But I now had a way to discard the tissues and underpants that I could not clean up. Wrap them in the abundant newspaper and roll it up like the rest. It would be many years before I knew that the "bandages" I saw were really sanitary napkins used by my mom and sisters.

Time to head home now. I must sit in the backseat in the farthest corner from Father Neary, as I was not quiet enough for him during today's "counseling" session. I was not being good enough for God to care for me. Next time I will do better, God, I promise.

On more than one occasion, when Father Neary picked me up, there were one or two other boys in the car. They were always in the backseat, while I got to sit up front. I would look over to the backseat, but as soon as we made eye contact we turned away from each other. We'd drive quietly to that same house. As we entered, there was a whole plate of cookies, a pitcher of milk, and glasses for all of us. We would sit and eat our cookies and drink our milk in silence. One by one, we would make the walk down the hallway to the back bedroom for our "counseling" sessions. We were in tune to the sounds, barely echoing faintly down the hall. If there was too much noise, then God would be angered. I don't know which was worse—waiting my turn, eating my cookies, and drinking my milk while I knew exactly what was going on down the hall, or being the first and getting it over? We never spoke to each other, except once, when one of them, teary-eyed and shaking, asked to share my tissues and toilet paper, as he had made a horrible error; he had left home without the required pockets full. I gave him all that I thought I could spare, as he began to tear up in fear. After that, I packed double in my pockets, just in case someone else needed some. The woman would sit and smile at us, telling us only that we were going to make good priests. *God, if I am to be holy at the end of this, then why does it feel so wrong? Maybe more is to come, and then I'll see.*

I arrive home, put on my happy face, and once again try to shut this out of my mind. My mind—that is the only place that is truly mine. My body has been ravaged by this man of the cloth, a Holy Roman Catholic Priest. My childhood has been ripped from me. My innocence is gone forever. *What lies ahead, God?* As I enter my house, Mom is there with a big grin on her face, asking me how the "counseling" went. I feebly reply that it went well and quickly head off to the bathroom, as I feel the warm, familiar feeling of blood leaking out. I must clean it up fast before it shows through my clothes. Drip, drip, drip. I sit there waiting for it to stop, and then I pack my bottom with tissues, just in case it starts again. I feel invisible to my family.

A detail of my abuse parallels others' experiences, I find out. "The range of abuse, were it not well documented, seems unbelievable. More than one priest 'anointed' his victim with semen, telling the victim the act had been sacred. Frequently the priest assures his victim that the behavior is holy and a special God-given gift. A frequently asked question is—how can a priest behave this way and carry on as a minister? Rationalization, denial, depersonalization, regression, and splitting are common" (Sipe 214).

9

DREAMS,
OR FADE TO BLACK?

To dream, to dreammmm. Even the word alone suggests something nice, sooth-ing, and enjoyable. It kind of rolls off your tongue, doesn't it? It's even fun to say. A pleasing experience. Then there are daydreams. These are the best, as you aren't asleep, but you are not fully awake or fully alert either. In a daydream, you can guide the course and outcome to some extent. You can stroll down a path you direct. You have a hand in the direction your daydream takes you. There is usu-ally a happy outcome. Then the next progression down the menu of dreams is the bad dream. A dream that you can't guide or intervene with. Unpleasant in nature and not something you want. You might wake up from a bad dream and remem-ber it then, but you might wake up later and forget it by morning. Bad dreams are the first stage of the journey downward to a deeper, darker place where you don't want to go, but you can't stop yourself. The next stage: nightmares.

Nightmares. The stuff scary movies are made of. You wish that nightmares would never happen. You wish that they would stop. You wish that you could intervene and not have nightmares. You feel out of control during the nightmare. Like a bad dream, you might remember a nightmare when you wake up from it but not remember it in the morning.

The next step, no, the next cliff, you fall off is night terrors. Night terrors are the granddaddy of bad dreams and nightmares. Night terrors make the worst slasher movies, the worst horror movies period, that you have ever seen or heard of seem like a trip to the park. Night terrors are the kind of thing that might even keep Stephen King awake at night and make him turn his lights on. Those of you holding this book right now who were raped by clergy know what I'm talking about. Night terrors are the monsters of all events that are outside of your con-trol.

Night terrors rock you to your very bone marrow. Down to the dark side of your faith and soul. The rest of this chapter is not for the weak of heart or the squeamish. If you can't handle it, stop here, and go to the next chapter. For those of you still with me, fasten your seat belts; it will be a bumpy ride from here on out.

Welcome to my world. The world where there are no rules, and there are no boundaries or limits. With night terrors, you bolt straight up sometimes. You are almost always covered in sweat from head to toe, and you feel clammy. You may yell as you awaken, and you may feel trapped by the covers as you wrestle to awaken yourself. I have kicked my poor wife on occasion, as I run in my terror-driven dream. My legs feel like I am running in knee-deep quicksand. Really, my legs are just tangled in the sheets, but until I awaken, it feels like I can't move and my legs are failing me as I run from the events in my night terror. You feel pain, life-ending pain. Sometimes paralyzed stiff, flat out on your back, you awaken but are unable to move for moments that feel like hours. You try to move your arms, legs, anything, but you are frozen in place. You know you are awake, but you can't move. Other times, you bolt awake in pain so intense that tears start to form uncontrollably and fall from your eyes instantly. You are out of breath, shaking, weak, sick to your stomach, feeling like you should make a mad dash for the bathroom for fear of vomiting in your bed. Life-crushing pain. You feel so helpless, so vulnerable. Now the stage is set. Last chance to skip this chapter.

OK, it's nighttime, early evening, a few hours to go to bed time. You hope tonight will be different, but you know you are hoping against hope. You begin to dread bedtime. You start to feel your stomach turn; you know what's coming tonight. It comes more nights than it doesn't. You lie in bed in the dark. You reach for your loved one next to you. In my case, Sue. You must touch skin. Even her hand. Hope begins to fade as your mate rolls away, asleep. She has inevitably fallen asleep. You are alone, and it is dark. You try your best to fall asleep and stay awake at the same time. You are tired, and your body craves sleep and rest; it demands it of you. You try not to give in and fall asleep because you know what lies ahead. Yet, you must give in at some point. Sometimes it is held off for hours as you fight yourself both to stay awake and go to sleep simultaneously. A personal war. You fill your head with pleasant memories, trying to fool yourself into laying the ground rules for a good dream, knowing you will lose the battle as you fall asleep. Will tonight bring the cold sweats, the running legs, the awakening to intense physical pain, the shaking, the bolting erect, or the paralyzed, rigid body? Maybe a combination of many of those. The nights you get off scot-free are becoming fewer and fewer. I am haunted from beyond the grave. Neary comes to me in the dark. I can feel his presence sometimes as I awake. He is dead, so how does he do this? If only you could dictate your dream content.

It is now early evening. I must stop my writing and begin my routine of planning how to get through tonight. Think pleasant thoughts, think pleasant thoughts. I will resume writing in the morning. Good night?

Well, you won't be disappointed. Last night was a breakthrough of sorts. Until last night, there has been a common thread to my night terrors. Without exception, they have either started at my childhood home in Camillus, New York, took place entirely there, or ended there. Nope, not last night. Neary's evil has invaded my current home, my bedroom, and the bed I share with my wife. How dare he? How does he reach from the grave and come to me? He has been dead for three years now, or has he? Does his soulless being still roam the dark recesses of the night? Is he too evil for even the Devil to let in? The Devil himself may draw the line at those who prey upon children.

I am asleep, yet I see shadows in my bedroom. Changes in the dark patterns around the room. The very low glow from the clock radio I see beyond the foot of the bed. What was that? Movement? A dark figure? A dark figure moving about the bedroom. It is he, I know it somehow. The furnace clicks on, and warm air rises next to my side of the bed. Then cold, very cold air overcomes me, even though I hear the furnace running. A tall, dark figure looms over me. It is he. The outline of his being is standing right there, right by my side. I feel my heart starting to race. My pulse quickening. I feel my chest rising and lowering. I am consciously aware of my breathing now. I exhale, and I see my breath as it leaves my mouth and rises toward his dark figure. It's almost as if he inhales the air I exhale, while at the same time I smell his tobacco-stained, bad breath, and the little bit of light reflects off of his yellow teeth as he grins. My chest is now pounding. I swear that my heart will come through my ribs. There is just enough light to reflect off his tiny bit of white collar, while his priestly garb of black is lost in the shadows. I am frozen, unable to move, unable to lift even a finger. I must wake Sue up. I must save her from this evil presence. She does not see him; she does not know he is here. I strain to move toward her, to cover and protect her. She is my true soul mate. She has been with me through all the bad and good times. Somehow I must shield her, but how? Panic! Move, damn it, move. Why am I still frozen? He is bending over me, getting ever closer. He is inhaling my breath and grinning like the Cheshire cat. Something shiny in his hands. I can only catch a glimpse as the dim light reflects off it. What is it? Move, damn it move, sit up, fight him off somehow, and defend yourself. What? I am now physically that ten-year-old boy, but I am fifty-three, aren't I? I see it. It is a saw. I see little shards of light as he lowers it over my throat. He is sawing, sawing my head off. Grinning all the time. I feel wet; it's my blood flowing everywhere. Then I feel *pain*, life-ending pain. I begin to ingest my own blood, as he reaches ever deeper into my neck. I try to breathe, only to swallow my own blood. I try to move. *Move*, damn it, move. The *pain*, the crippling pain. Warm liquid, my blood, is leaving me, draining me, and my life is fading. Intense pain. I hear him almost giggling as he leans harder into the saw. My bones, my spinal cord, I can feel my head becoming detached from my body. *Sue! Sue!* Help me. Wake up and help me, somehow.

The blood flows into my eyes, and they become blurry. I begin to rise above myself. I am above him, looking down, as if floating near the ceiling somehow. My body below me watches as he continues separating my head from my body. I see my legs begin to move, my arms too. My body becomes limp. He holds my head like a prize. Does he have others? Am I the only one? How can I still be here, as I look at my headless body in a pool of blood?

This must be it. I am dying. It is my soul I'm looking down with. My soul has left my body and is hovering over my headless body that lies so still. Why do I still feel so much pain? Why does it hurt so much?

Where is the warm white light we have been told about since childhood? Where is an angel, or God, to take me into the light? I am dying, but there is no comfort, and no sense of warmth, no sense of walking toward the light. It is getting darker, darker, and darker. Is there no God? Am I really so damaged, so evil too, for what this priest did to me? That I stopped fighting to free myself? Everywhere around me is almost totally black. I feel myself slipping away, fading away. No light, no warmth—just blackness, blackness everywhere I look, everywhere I turn. Then nothing, nothing, and I cease to exist. It is over, I am done, a headless ten-year-old in the body of a fifty-three-year-old. It is finally over. Will there be peace?

I'm fighting my way to sit up. My arms and legs begin to move. I gasp for air, trying to breathe. It is Sue and she is telling me it's OK and she is here. She tells me to wake up. I'm not dead? I am alive? How? I just died, and all went black. Sue shakes me a little, wraps her arms around my trembling body, and tells me that she is here. She holds me, trying to stop the shaking, trembling man she has called her soul mate, her husband, for years. I still shake, still gasp for air. Each time I try to inhale, it takes much effort. I slowly become aware that I am here, and that I am not dead.

Now awake, listening to Sue, feeling her embrace, my breathing becomes more normal. All is well? I tell her that "he" was here; "he" was taking my life.

Somehow reaching out from the grave. She holds me and drifts back off to sleep. I lie there, awake. Staring into the dark, the shadows, wondering if he will be back tonight. Is it safe to go to sleep? If I give in to sleep, will I die? Am I dead now and dreaming that I am still here? Will I awaken in the morning? As I lie there, wrestling in my mind, time passes, and I lose the battle to stay awake. Later, morning comes once again.

Sleep well tonight. Don't look into the shadows around your room. Or maybe you should. You were let off easy. This was one of my tamer nighttime terror dreams. It was, however, the first one that played out in my bedroom where we now live and not at my childhood home. Neary is expanding his universe, reaching out from a dead, evil place.

If you're still here, our journey resumes. You have been duly warned. In this night terror, I am ten years old, back at my childhood home. It is cloudy and overcast, a bit cool for summer. Neary is humping my little anus for all he is worth. He is very fast and rough today. How many times will he visit me this week? As he finishes, after climaxing, he takes some of my tissues to clean the blood and semen off himself. I am bleeding more than usual. I feel the warm blood run down my legs and drip to the floor. I can't stop the bleeding this time. This time there is a tremendous pain. I am totally naked, still leaning over my bed. He has already zipped up his pants, and he has a huge grin on his face. You can feel the evil emanating from him; it is like an aura of sorts. The room feels cold, very cold, but it is in the seventies outside, and my window is open. The cold is coming from Neary somehow. His eyes look like two black pools; there are no discernable pupils.

I run from my room, totally naked. A red trail of blood follows me. I don't care this time. I look over my shoulder, and he is coming for me. "Clean yourself up!" he shouts, "or you will die. I will see to it." I make a hurried rush down the stairs, my bloody trail behind every step. My legs move too slowly, and he is getting closer. Ever closer. What is wrong with my legs? They feel so heavy, like in quicksand of some sort. I make it into the living room. There are my siblings, watching television. I appeal to them. I try to touch them, shake them, and make them see me. Neary is directly behind, and he laughs, telling me that they can't help me. I even stand directly in front of the TV, and they still can't hear me or see me. Why? I see my dad sitting in the corner of the room, reading the newspaper. I approach him. I grab for the paper, trying to pull it from his hands. My little ten-year-old hands only wash through the newspaper. I frantically try to get his attention. No. Nothing is working. Neary begins to smile from ear to ear, as he taunts me, saying, "No one can help you. They don't even see you."

I brush past Neary on my way to the kitchen. My mom is in the kitchen. Surely she will stop him. Somehow, Neary gets there ahead of me and is standing next to my mom. He again breaks into laughter, with that big smile. Blood is everywhere. There is so much blood that I am slipping on it as it spills onto the kitchen floor. "Mom! Mom!" I scream. I try to touch her. She is there, but does not respond to my efforts. She is singing to herself, humming to herself, and she appears to be happy. Father Neary is upstairs, making her son into a priest.

My dad and mom's bedroom is right off the kitchen. In there, I know there is a shotgun, my dad's shotgun, in the closet at the far corner of the room. I make my way to his closet, open the door, and reach in for the shotgun. I grab it by the barrel and pull it out of the closet. As I turn around, he is right there, smiling, laughing, and reminding me that I will die if I tell anyone. The shotgun is almost as tall as I am, and he is so big, standing in the middle of the room. Telling me I am going to die.

My dad was safety conscious, and the gun and shells are stored separately. But where? Where are the bullets, the shells? Dragging the shotgun behind me I search for the shotgun shells. I frantically pull my dad's drawers open. Are they in his dresser? Are they on a shelf nearby? I cannot find them anywhere. Neary taunts me with, "It doesn't matter, they won't hurt me. God is with me. God protects me. You're wasting your time, and only delaying your death by minutes." Neary is enjoying the entire, fruitless struggle I am having, and he continues to laugh. His dead, dark eyes pierce me to my very soul and beyond.

Success! I find a box of bullets in a nightstand next to the window. I open the box, fumbling to find the right bullets for the shotgun. There are none. Each one I pick up is either too big or too small. There are bullets in there, but no shotgun shells. I look down at the floor, and it is entirely covered with blood, my blood. I begin to slip and fall. Am I going to die, as Neary tells me? I make a desperate attempt to hit him with the shotgun. He laughs as it passes right through him, his laughs getting louder as he approaches me. I slip in a pool of my blood and am on my back, naked, covered in blood. Neary comes to me, with those unforgettable yellow teeth in a big smile and bad breath. Where are the shotgun shells? I still think, if only …

I am flat on my back, arms outstretched, one to the left, and one to the right. The same position Jesus was in when he was nailed to the cross before they raised it upright and placed it in the hole. *God, are you here with me? Help me! Please help me!*

Neary sits on my little chest. He is heavy, and it is very hard for me to breathe. He places one knee on each of my arms, pinning me down. I struggle; against all hope I struggle. I cry for my mom or dad, "Help me, Help me." No one is coming. No one hears or sees me except for Father Neary. I feel his hands as they slide around my neck. He begins to choke me, not fast, but very slowly. He wants me to suffer for a long time. He oscillates between very tight and loose enough for me gasp a short breath. Neary wants to prolong my death to make sure I suffer enough. He remains on my chest. I feel his penis getting hard against my belly. He is really enjoying this. He chokes me and begins to rock back and forth, rubbing his penis on my belly.

God, please end my life. Let me die; even if you send me to Hell, let me die. Should I be asking the Devil to take me, as you don't answer my prayers for this to stop? I begin to fade. I feel darkness setting in. I float up from the floor and hover at ceiling height, looking down, as my trapped, little body gets weaker by the second. I see Neary's body stiffen up as he climaxes on my belly. I am back in my body, almost void of life. His eyes look down on me, his grin all too familiar. I again leave my body and am hovering at ceiling level, looking down on him and myself.

Darkness begins to overtake me. I no longer can breathe. I can no longer move even a finger. I am motionless. My eyes are still glued to him as he rises and stands over me like I am a trophy he has won. Yes, he was right. I am dying. My little, ten-year-old boy's body is going completely limp. He smiles and says, "I told you that you would die."

Against the ceiling, I feel darkness closing in on me. Everything is getting dim, but I still hear him laughing. Soon enough, there is total darkness—the fade to black. Where is the white light? Where is the warm glow, the angel to take me to God and Heaven? I am becoming cold, very cold. It's getting so dark. I cry out, *God, please help me.* But, as in my prayers, my call goes unanswered. So very cold now, so very dark.

I no longer can see anything but darkness. I can move freely, though, with no restraint. However, I do not move. I am in some kind of total blackness. I've never seen such emptiness, nor have I dreamed of such. I move my arms, my legs. I scream, but nothing comes out. It is just getting darker. This is the end, but there is no white light and warmth, as I was told.

Now, even the darkness is closing in. I feel myself getting ever so smaller, almost as if I were being erased somehow. I fade to black; I no longer exist in any form. It is over, finally over—or is it?

I bolt straight up. I am covered in sweat. I feel clammy, weak, almost dizzy. Sue reaches out to me. She strokes my head. "It is OK, I am here, Charley. You are safe." Am I alive, or is this part of the nighttime terror? As the moments pass,

I realize that I am truly still here. Sue continues to comfort me. She gently holds me.

This bastard not only haunts me, but brings my wife into it. He reaches from beyond the grave and not only touches me, but also Sue.

OK, put the book down. Go get a glass of water. Take a few minutes break. I will be here when you come back. The night terrors will be here when you return. They haunt me during my waking hours when I try to rest. If I'm busy, they seem to wait for the first moment I get to rest. Then they take over and come back. These aren't a onetime event. They repeat themselves over and over, getting worse with each "repeat," as they play out in my head and return when I sleep. You're getting off easy still, as the worst ones I won't even share with myself.

In this night terror, it is a nice, sunny, warm day. We are at my family's home. It sits on about two acres of land, of which we mow a little over half. My younger brother and I used to mow it with those gas powered, reel-type mowers. He on one, me on the other. My dad would get us started early in the day, as the mowers only cut about a twenty-inch path.

I smell the freshly cut grass. I feel the warmth of the sun. I see all my family out in the yard, the backyard by the porch. I am in the side yard, as they make their way around toward me. They all seem happy, and they all talk among themselves. My dad, however, is in his bathrobe, while everyone else is dressed. Why? His robe is partly opened. I gaze at him as he is only bones—no flesh, just bones. I yell out to them, as I am only a few feet away. They don't hear me. They talk to each other and to Dad. Can't they see that he is only a skeleton? Am I the only one who can see this? How do they not see that they are there, and he is not? Why do I see him as I do?

I strain to get up and look. I am facedown in the grass, my head turned to one side. I feel the grass clippings that were left behind, and I smell their strong odor. I can't move. Why? I am naked, lying facedown on the grass. No one hears me call, although they are only a few feet away. I see my dad look my way, and his skull nods like he can hear me. Somehow he knows I am there, but no one else does, and no one else sees him the way I do.

I try to get up. I try to move, but I can't. Why? What is happening? I feel pressure, a weight on my arms. They are outstretched to my side. I can't turn my head enough to see their faces. I only see black shoes, black slacks. As I strain to look, I feel pain. These people are standing on my arms, and someone is holding my feet. I manage to turn my head to the opposite side, and there he is, grinning, standing there with the ever present pipe, his yellow teeth showing, his bad breath reaching down to me.

What is happening? Who are the other men dressed in black, as he is? He bends down, on one knee, and he begins to speak Latin, and the others join in. I don't know what they are saying. The pain begins to build from their weight on my arms and the holding of my legs. As I write this in real time, I am beginning to feel real pain—how can this be?

Neary kneels at my side. He has a razor blade knife, which he proudly shows me, still grinning. I see him move it out of view. What is he going to do this time? I leave my body and watch from above, floating just a few feet above us all. I now see that he has brought three other priests to aid him today. There is a priest holding each arm, and one is holding my feet. I begin to choke on some freshly cut grass clippings, but how? I am facedown on the ground and hovering over myself at the same instant.

I see and feel Neary trace my back carefully. He is using some kind of marker. He traces the outline of a cross on my back. It is about three inches wide, running the length of my spine. He then draws the crosspiece about three inches wide also, from shoulder to shoulder. He then stands back up, as if he is admiring his work so far. More Latin is heard from the four of them.

He bends down once more in the newly cut grass, and his breath is so bad that it overpowers the smell of the grass. I look toward my family only a few feet away. "Help me!" I cry. "Somebody help me!" Then I see her. My wife, Sue, is standing but a few feet in front of me. She is being held on both sides by two more men in priestly garb. What is about to happen? I see Sue's tears flowing down her cheeks, as she pleads for him to stop. She struggles to get free and is only retained all the tighter by her captors. I hear her screaming, and she hears me yelling for them to let her go. Neary says, "No, you have broken the rules. You have disclosed our times together. You have violated the rules, and now you will receive your punishment."

I look down from above. I see all of them: my family who doesn't see me there, my wife who continues to plead to be released, and then me. I am again that little ten-year-old boy on the ground, facedown with a cross drawn on my back. However, the floating person above is me at my current age. I look down at my little self. I must intervene somehow—but how?

All my efforts prove fruitless. I watch from above, as he kneels at my side. I feel the razor knife begin to cut my flesh as he traces the cross on my back. Warm blood flows from the cuts. He has barely started when I scream and pass out. He stops, and he waits. He waits until I wake up again. I am to be awake for this. It is my punishment, he tells me. It cycles many times. He cuts, then I scream, look at Sue, and pass out. When I awaken, he starts to cut again. Eventually, he is done.

The outline of the cross is cut into my little body. Is it over? Will he let me go this time? Have I suffered enough?

He pulls the cross made of flesh from my body. He holds it up like some kind of trophy. I hear the other priests speaking loudly in Latin. I look down from above. I see the cross made of skin, the red exposed underflesh of my body where the cross was lifted out.

They let me go. I think they might believe that I am dead, but I am not. I am both facedown in the grass and up here a few feet above them. Neary takes his razor knife and begins to cut pieces from my fleshy cross and pass some to each of his fellow priests. Once again, more Latin is spoken, more words that I can't understand. They look like they are offering it up somehow, and then they begin to ingest my flesh. The blood is dripping from the corners of their mouths as they all grin at the same time.

I stir; Neary looks down on me and is surprised by my little movement. He reaches into his pocket and takes out a small container. What is it? What is he going to do now? Soon enough I find out. It is salt. He begins to shake it over the formation of the cross on my back. I scream like I never thought anyone could scream. My little self on the ground and my adult self hovering above both scream. Unbelievable pain. I pass out. My floating self watches as they devour the fleshy cross. Sue has passed out from the horror she has just witnessed. She comes to, and moves to me. Her tears cover and wash my face free of my own blood. The priests seem oblivious to me and her now.

The priests finish their feast and hold Sue once again. She is at my head, and they once again restrain me too. I am getting weaker by the second from the blood loss. I can feel myself slipping away, ever so slowly. Father Neary now takes out a little drill type instrument from his pocket. It is some kind of saw. I hear it start up, and he begins to saw my exposed ribs and spinal column. I feel my life ending, and I feel life-ending pain. I look to Sue, and think how I hurt for her.

I smell the burning of my ribs as he cuts. The pain is intense. Somehow I let go. I give into the pain, the smells, and his breath.

One again, darkness is setting in. The sky above me is getting darker and farther away. I feel my life ebbing away. I stop breathing. I stop moving, as he happily saws away. The pain is going away, the darker it gets. The light. Where is the light? Where is the warmth of that white light? You know, the one we have been told about all our lives—the one that dying people tell us about. It is not here. Only darkness. I feel cold, very cold, getting weaker and darker by the second.

Then there is nothing. Absolutely nothing. Total darkness. Once again, I move, but to where? There is no up, no down, no sideways—only the darkness. I feel myself being absorbed into this nothing. I fade away. There is no sign of me.

Severe pain! I bolt up once again. Sue is not there. Where is she? I flail around the bed, "Help me Sue. Where are you?" Am I truly dead and gone? Your side of the bed is empty. Am I awake, or am I reaching out from the darkest of dark to you? I feel sick. I may throw up. I untangle my feet from the bed sheets and try to sit up. I feel pain, real bad pain, in my back.

As I continue to awaken, I begin to remember. Sue is in the other room, asleep. She was coming down with a cold and wanted to spare me from it. She is so wonderful, but she is also on the list of casualties caused by an evil man. Not sick a man—no—an evil man.

My pulse begins to slow. I am alive; I didn't die after all. At least not this time. Our youngest son took some psychology courses at college, and he learned about dreams and their meanings. He said that people who die in their dreams do sometimes die for real. For now, I am safe?

If you have made it this far, then you have a small glimpse of my world at night. Almost each and every night. There are a series of these nighttime terrors that come to me in the night. These are only the "tip of the iceberg." There are many more night terrors with even more evil than what you have read today.

Wouldn't it be nice if we could somehow direct our dreams? I look continuously to find a way to stop these, but they still plague me almost each and every night. There is one tool that Dr. Driscoll gave me that at times helps. However it is twofold. First, I replay the horror just before falling asleep, and I force my adult self to intervene and stop it. I alter it for a different outcome. I try to force the way I would want it to end.

I have had some luck in this department. However, after playing it out in my head and changing the outcome, I am still left with the conflict of both trying to fall asleep and fighting to stay awake to avoid the possible night terror. I have run the latest terror through my head and fixed the content and outcome. That being said, there are so many terrors, that it may be a different rerun tonight, or a whole new one. They are nightly battles, which I lose more than I win.

Hmmmm … smell that? Sniff, sniff. You smell that? Don't you? Sniff, sniff. I know that smell. Sniff, sniff. I feel fear setting in. I sense that I am shaking a little. Sniff, sniff … it can't be. I feel my heart starting to accelerate, faster, faster, sniff, sniff. No, he is dead, isn't he? I am dreaming, right? I will wake up now. Wake up! Wake up! OK, sniff, sniff, it is he. You can smell it, right? His pipe tobacco. None other like it. Open your eyes. You're sleeping! Sniff, sniff, how is this possible? I open my eyes slowly. There he is! Hovering over me about two feet above me. Grinning, smirking, and puffing on his ever present pipe. "Hello Charles, it is I, and I'm here for you."

All though I am still asleep, I dreamed I was awake. "Sue! Sue, wake up! Wake up, Sue! It's him! He's here, floating over me about two feet above me." I'm awake, so why can't I wake up my wife? Why does she not smell the smoke, and why can she not hear me call to her? I see her lying next to me, where she always is. Maybe if I shake her? "Sue, Sue, wake up, help me!" I now feel sweat dripping off me onto the sheets. I look up, and he's still there. "Charles, I have come for you." Sniff, sniff. Sue, Sue, I am shaking you, wake up wake up! "It won't work, Charles. No one will come. No one will save you. It's just you and me." I see his yellow teeth, stained from years of tobacco use. I see the ever present grin, an evil grin, and there is cold emanating from him. I reach up and feel colder, the closer my hands reach out toward him. "Yes, it's me, and I've come for you. You'll join me in hell for all eternity. We'll be together forever. You and I Charles. It's time." No! No! I am lifting off the bed. Coming closer toward him and feeling colder too. I flail my arms about and kick my feet. How can this be? He is dead, dead for over two years. I try to turn and look down toward Sue. She is sleeping peacefully. "Say good-bye to her, Charles. You will be with me from this moment on."

I bolt straight up! I'm covered with sweat, shaking, breathing heavily, heart pounding. Sue notices. It's OK, Charley, it's OK. I'm here." I begin to weep. I tell Sue, "He was just here, wasn't he?" I frantically look around the dimly lit bedroom, my eyes darting to every shadow, every dark corner. Sue reassures me, softly stroking my head, telling me he is not here, and telling me that he is dead.

Once more, one more night, I battle to go to sleep and stay awake at the same time. When I drift off, I know what lies ahead. I feel clammy already. *Please God, not tonight. Let this night be pain free. Let me remember nothing in the morning, and let me sleep undisturbed.* Nice thought, but, no, it wasn't to be. It is cold, a crisp fall day. Sunny, but with that clear edge to the air. All the leaves are on the ground. A light breeze kisses my cheeks, and gives me a little pink color. The fallen leaves make their symphony of sounds, as they are tossed about by the wind. I hear them crunch underfoot as I approach the water's edge. The lake looks sullen, darker, with only small ripples, as if from a skipping stone that has sunk. The lake is readying itself for the coming winter and the ice cap.

As I get closer to the shore, I see something that doesn't fit the picture. There, about halfway out the length of the pier is a red floating object. As I near the waters edge, I see movement. Do I? What is in the water? Other people notice too as they walk the lakeshore and start in my direction. A few run out onto the pier. I hear them shout, "It's a body." Without any hesitation, I enter the water. I don't feel the cold, as people yell to me to stop. I move only faster, as they cry for me to stop because the water is too cold, and the red object in the water is almost neck deep. All of a sudden, instantly, the cold hits me all at once. Instantly, I feel cold from my chest to my feet. As I reach the floating red object, I see. It is a young boy, maybe eight to ten years old. As I grab him, I notice that he is pale, so very pale. It was as if he had been in the water a long time. I try to make it over to the pier to hand him off to those on the pier, but the water level is too low to be able to reach up that high.

I return to my swim toward the shore, as I hear the bystanders yelling. They are all yelling at once, and I cannot hear the words, as each one yells over the next. As I near the shore and begin to lift him up out of the water, I feel the rigidness of his small limbs. I see the bruises about his head. His little legs are exposed because his pants are gone, but his socks remain. I lay him on the shore, as people gather around. I stroke his little head, as I begin to weep uncontrollably. He begins to look familiar to me.

Then his eyes pop open, and he grabs my arm. As I look into his eyes, I see. It is I. It is I at age ten. I scan the faces in the crowd. Do they not see him open his eyes? Do they not see him grab my arm? How can they not see when it is right in front of them? He pulls me to his chest and whispers in my ear, "It was Father Neary. He did this to me and is back at the rectory packing his bag right now to leave on an unscheduled vacation." The boy begs me to go to the rectory and stop Father Neary. The boy is me. No one else sees this boy as I do. It is me at the time of the death of my childhood, a tender young boy of ten. I cover him with my coat, as I run off toward the rectory, leaving his care, my care, to others at the scene.

I run the few blocks to the rectory. Out of breath, I ring the bell. I pound on the door, but I don't wait for an answer. I burst through the unlocked door, and there he is. All in his black garb, suitcase in hand, grinning at me and saying, "You're too late to save the boy, Charles. He has already passed." And then pain awakens me, and I look around. I am home. I am in my bed, with my loving wife beside me, and I lie back down.

My biggest fear? We all have one—one that is clearly the biggest by any scale that you could measure. What's your biggest fear? Come on, it's only you and me here. No one will know, just you and me. Go ahead. Say to yourself, *my biggest fear is* … I guess my biggest fear would be to die in my sleep, in the arms of a night terror. That is my biggest fear. To pass in the night, some say that is a good way to go. Me? Not in the throes of a night terror. That passing is the most terrifying thing I can imagine. The stress would cause my heart to stop, while lying next to Sue, and I would not be able to hug her one last time or give her one last kiss before exiting this world.

Exit to what? Is this it? Is there really an afterlife? Do we truly know? Come on, admit it. You don't really know, do you? We have been told, many, many times. There is the reward of Heaven after our life on Earth is over. Do we really know, though? Not really. No one can say with 100 percent certainty that there is more. We hang on to this idea as a comfort. Live a good life, accept God, obey the Ten Commandments, believe in God, and you will be rewarded with your pass to Heaven and eternal happiness. Or don't, and burn in Hell for all time, until God does away with the Devil and all those souls in Hell. We beg for this to be true because we want more than this life has to offer. We need to believe in a reward after the end. We need to believe that the evil ones of this Earth will be duly punished in the afterlife, especially if they escaped any accountability for their crimes on Earth. We want to believe that if we play by the rules and follow God's teachings, then we will get our space in Heaven. We have all heard of the white light, the warm white light, the feeling of peace, of someone greeting us and taking us by hand into Heaven. Has this been programmed into us? Is this the way we know it will be, or the way we wish it to be? I desperately hope it is true, I want Father Neary to pay for the deeds he committed while on this Earth, parading around as God's priest—who never had his "feet held to the fire" when he walked this Earth. I want him enveloped in eternal flames for all those he harmed.

I want the afterlife to be true; I need it to be true. I hope God looks down at me and is not sickened by what I was forced to do as a child. I pray that my soul is not forever tainted by the evil things Neary made me do when I was ten years old. *God, forgive me for what I was forced to do as a child. Are you there? Hello?*

10

PUT IT BEHIND YOU

Put it behind you,
It was so long ago,
Just forget about it,
Move on.

All the words of a nonvictim who hasn't walked a step in my shoes, much less a mile. Everyone sexually abused by clergy would agree with me that moving on is not possible. I have spoken to many, many victims. The suggestion to "move on" is used freely by nonvictims. They have no idea how that suggestion hurts—or maybe they do? The Catholic Church uses so many of those types of lines too. They refer to the sexual rape of children as "inappropriate behavior," "inappropriate contact," a "mistake," or as (the worst I've ever heard so far) "mischief" by a priest. Funny, as a victim and survivor of sexual abuse, I take great exception to being referred to by the Church as a "mistake." I am not a mistake! A mistake to me and fellow victims means getting off the highway at the wrong exit, or turning left when you should have turned right. Or using a cup of sugar and not a teaspoon. Those are mistakes—the rape of a little child is not a mistake!

The release of the "audit" presented by the National Review Board (a watchdog group of lay Catholics appointed by the Church) and the John Jay College of Criminal Justice in January of 2004 was a great letdown for victims of abuse by priests. The "audit," as they called it, of the Catholic Church was actually only a voluntary self-study, as any rational person could see. It was not an audit, although they tried to pass it off as one. A truly independent audit would not have been comprised of people selected by and paid by the Church.

Everywhere I have researched it, I have read that anal intercourse performed on a young boy by a man in his forties (much less a Catholic priest) is illegal. It is a crime, and it should not just be labeled as simply a mistake or mischief. It is not only a crime, but it is a felony crime. That is, it seems, unless you belong to the

Catholic Church. Father Tom Doyle has just finished a book that traces the Catholic Church's knowledge of this evil over the last 2,000 years. The abuse is neither new nor unknown to the Church, and it is not a problem limited to the United States, as the Pope has played it to be. It happens worldwide. I heard Father Doyle speak once and he stated that his research indicates for every one of us who discloses our abuse, there are at least sixty who don't.

These people, who utter those ignorant words, *Put it behind you, It was so long ago, Just forget about it, Move on,* and many other hurtful words, just don't get it. I sometimes feel they have "chosen ignorance," as I have dubbed it. They cannot allow themselves to believe the facts, of the sexual abuse by clergy, because then they would have to admit to the abuse done by their priests to countless children. These Catholics can't seem to handle the truth. Otherwise, they would be as outraged at their church as the victims are. They would be demanding more of their church leaders to stop the abuse and hold those guilty accountable.

It is so hurtful to say "put it behind you" (an ironic choice of words, don't you think?) or "it was so many years ago." I live with this vile evil every day. I never can tell what might trigger me into a flashback, taking me right back there as if it had happened just a few moments before. For those of you who have not been raped by a priest, I would like to explain that the effects never go away. The best that victims can hope for is to remove some of the pain associated with the abuse. Abuse hurts most victims right down to their souls. We have been violated physically, emotionally, and spiritually, and we feel unworthy of God's love. We feel dirty, ashamed, guilt ridden, and embarrassed; we feel like damaged goods. Forget it? Put it behind you? How? There seems to be no end to the ignorant things that people will say. Don't they know that it would be a dream come true to do what they ask? If we could just move on, don't they think that we would? The effects live just below the surface, each and every minute of each and every day of our lives. We spend much time in search of ways to ease the pain.

Think of it in these terms, for the sake of argument: suppose I were to cut off one of your legs. Years pass, and we meet again. Have you forgotten it? Have you put it behind you? Why not? It's been a long time, it's been years, so just forget it and put it behind you. Why does it still bother you? Because every time you get up, walk, or move, you think about it in some fashion, don't you? My scars are the same, but are not as visible to the naked eye as the loss of a leg. However, given a choice, I know that I would choose the loss of a leg over being held down by a "Holy Roman Catholic Priest" who said he was "doing God's will" to me.

How about those of you who are old enough to remember or who were part of the Holocaust? That was many years ago. Have you forgotten? Have you put it behind you? I think not. Otherwise, why would we hear from time to time how a perpetrator of that evil is found and brought to trial? We are continually looking for justice. That's all any one of the victims/survivors I have met want. Justice. Simple justice. The chance to tell a jury exactly what happened to us.

Strange too, how there exists no statute of limitations on murder. Years passing mean nothing to a murder case. The victim can't be there for the trial either. But I am here, and I can testify as to what, where, and how it happened. Isn't that a leg up on a murder trial? We want our "day in court." However, the Catholic Church runs out to the private sector and hides behind the statute of limitations. What happened to separation of church and state? Does that apply only when it is convenient for the Church? How can they have it both ways?

I grew up Catholic and remember being told numerous times about doing the "right thing." Be honest and truthful. We have all heard the "what would Jesus do" saying. I find it hard to believe that Jesus would hide behind a civil statute to protect these child rapists. As a matter of fact, I think the Jesus to whom I pray stated it very clearly in the Bible, in Matthew 18:1–6. It reads as follows:

> At that time, the disciples came to Jesus, saying, "Who is the greatest in the Kingdom of Heaven?" And calling to him a child, he put him in the midst of them and said, "Truly, I say to you, unless you turn and become like children, you will never enter the Kingdom of Heaven. Whoever humbles himself like this child, he is the greatest in the Kingdom of Heaven. Whoever receives one such child in my name receives me; but whoever causes one of these little ones who believe in me to sin, it would be better for him to have a great millstone fastened round his neck and to be drowned in the depth of the sea."

Gee, it sounds painfully simple how Jesus feels about those who rape children, not limited to only priests. It reads to me that he not only despises their actions, but believes in capital punishment for it. No one I've ever heard of could stay afloat with a millstone around his or her neck. How about you? Read about the early Catholic Church, say AD 300, and you will see that priests who harmed little ones were executed.

I know. I can hear you repeating the Church's weak argument about how it's a societal problem. Yes, it is. However, these predator priests were moved from church to church, parish to parish, not unlike chess pieces and we victims were their chessboard. My perpetrator was in scores of churches, most of which have had someone contact me about his sexual rapes. The statistics as they now stand report that many priests harm hundreds of "little ones" over their forty- or fifty-year career. I know that Neary committed abuse over more than forty years, as there are victims older than I and as young as their middle twenties. Out in society, there exists no relocation program for sex offenders. Once caught, they are hauled away and locked up, pending an investigation.

I tire of being told to forgive. I must agree with this: "Forgiveness is a venerable religious ideal that can, however, be used as a defense against accepting the reality, accountability, and etiology of abuse. Reconciliation is operative only when one accepts full responsibility for transgressions, establishes reforms, and makes restitution. This is true for an abuser, a diocese, or community" (Sipe 256).

An auxiliary bishop once said that he knew it was a sin, (the sexual abuse of children), but until recently, wasn't sure it was against the law. We were not born yesterday. What vacuum has he lived in? In his reign of several decades, we are supposed to believe that he never once watched TV or read the newspaper and never saw a person arrested for this crime? That is yet another insult thrown at us. I truly thought that "ignorance of the law is no excuse." Doesn't that apply to all of us?

11

THERE WAS SOMETHING SPECIAL ABOUT MY WIFE, SUE

There was something special about my wife. I felt it, and she felt that I was special too. It had to do with eye contact mostly. Our eyes would kind of lock on each other during our high school years, when we saw each other from time to time. We always noticed each other in the halls of West Genesee High School. Even though we never spoke to each other, we were very aware that there was a definite connection there—something not tangible, but there nonetheless.

I had pretty much dated the same girl all though high school. Sue, however, was way different. She dated and had many different boyfriends. She says she didn't feel a strong commitment to any of them. Sue wasn't one to take things that seriously.

I remember the junior prom. I went with my date, and Sue went with hers. Sue says she kept an eye on us because my date and she had the same dress on. You just couldn't help but notice. I even spent time working at her boyfriend's dad's place selling Christmas trees one year. He would speak of Sue.

I started to notice her getting on and off the bus; I now confess that she had dynamite legs. Great legs. Sue would go to the back of the bus with the smokers, even though she did not smoke, and I would be in the front of the bus with my books, always doing what was right. We seemed miles apart, but our eyes always connected. I went off to college and married my high school girlfriend. Sue didn't marry her date from the prom. She met a different guy from high school, and they were married. Both of us married too young and—long story short—both marriages failed. We both thought we would live happily ever after with our chosen spouses, never thinking of divorce. Then, one day while Sue and I were grocery shopping with our spouses, we saw each other in the store. Sue had a little boy, their son, with her. Once again, our eyes did what they had always done. They connected again after so many years. We had never even said as much as hello to each other—that's what makes the connection so odd. That day, we said a simple hi. I don't think either of our spouses even knew that we had spoken. Some how, on some level, I knew that she wasn't happy. I could tell by her eyes and how she looked at me. I knew that I wasn't happy either. My wife wanted college and a career, and there was little, if any, room for children, which broke my heart. I knew that I could be such a good father, but I guessed that that might never happen. I'd never get that chance, because I did not believe in divorce. So I needed to make the best of a bad situation. Besides, I thought that maybe someday I would be able to change her mind. Sue and I put each other out of mind once more. I went home, wondering what her life was like. I had no idea that Sue's life was falling apart. Her husband didn't keep any job for very long, and Sue soon moved back in with her parents to try and start over.

My life, too, was changing and falling apart. My wife informed me that she needed some "space." She started coming home later and later each day. Then, one day I came home from work, and she was gone. She, too, had gone back to her parents, as Sue had done. I called her parents' house, and was told that she needed some time to think. A few days later, I received paperwork from her attorney about a divorce. I had thought, before she left, that I would let her calm down and everything would be OK, then the mail came. It was over; our brief marriage was to end in divorce.

Once again, I felt defeated by life—first the priest abuse and then a failed marriage. What more could happen to me, and how much more could I take? A childhood friend came over to cheer me up one night, and he convinced me to go with him to a nightclub. He said he knew one not far, and had met a girl there himself. I didn't want to go out, and I didn't feel up to it, but I went. We were just sitting around, and I was just feeling bad about what had happened. My friend was soon talking to girls. Then, out of nowhere, Sue walked over and said, "Don't I know you from the school bus when we were in high school?" I said yes really fast. She had a guy with her, and they both sat down to talk.

Then she asked me to ask her to dance. She asked me, while we were dancing, if I could help her either ditch or get rid of the guy she was with. She had just met him, and he wouldn't leave her alone. I said that I would help, and I asked him to leave when we got back to the table. I then asked her who she had been out with that night, and she said she was with her girlfriends. I offered to drive her home. We had spent years living only a few streets apart. Even when she moved to Camillus, we were only a few streets apart, really less than a five-minute walk. As children, we were at the same playgrounds, and we sledded on the same hill, known as Westcott Reservoir, maybe even at the same time. Sue feels that a higher power kept us in close proximity—maybe it was fate.

That night, I knew exactly where to drive her home. When we arrived at her home, she asked me in for a few minutes to see a dress she had just bought. I turned to leave and kissed her, and she didn't seem to mind. Our eyes locked again in silence. I also could not help but tell her that I was going to marry her. I'm not sure what she thought, but I was sure of it; somehow I knew. She laughed, and I left. I think I scared her just a little. I started to send her flowers, and I spent a lot of time with her son, Lee, who was about eighteen months old at the time. Lee grew to love me, and so did Sue. Sue and I became the best of friends. One day, her friend told her that if Sue wasn't really interested in me, then her friend would want to date me. Sue started to think. Hey, wait a minute here; maybe she needed to think about what she might be losing.

It was Christmastime and Sue called me and asked if we could go look at friendship rings to give to each other as gifts. When we arrived at the jewelry store, she went directly over to the diamonds (talk about a woman with a plan!). We looked at the engagement rings together. And left the store with a ring. I planned to take Sue out for a nice dinner and propose properly. Sue, once again, had plans of her own. So there we were, sitting in my car in the parking garage, and Sue told me it would be OK to give it to her right then. I told her my plan, but we both got caught up in the moment, and I proposed in the parking garage.

A new beginning, a new start—it felt so right this time. I could see myself growing old with this wonderful woman. A new life for me with the girl I had always wanted and would always love. What could be better? I wanted eight children, and she wanted four. She won, but I know now why I wanted eight. I have always loved commotion; the more exhausted I was, the more I would fall into deep sleep and not think or even dream. I had work and school when I took classes, and our kids were involved in a lot of activities too. Football, soccer, cheerleading, marching band, piano lessons, tennis—you name it, and our children did it. They were lucky enough to be able to participate in many things. I still lock eyes with her to this day, and melt when she comes to me. It is magic—pure magic.

12

FATHERS

Father's Day, 2004. This Sunday is Father's Day. While I am the father of four adults who are building their own lives, I seem to reflect on my dads. I use the term "dads," because I was blessed with two of them. One, my biological dad, and the other I won in a jackpot, by marriage to the most wonderful woman God created. If I sound like I'm bragging, well I am. My father-in-law, Gerry, is now dead just over two years. My biological dad is now gone eight years. Still, every once in a while, I cannot not help but feel their presence and their influence on me as I carve my space on this planet. I wished I could have told them how I felt when they were here among us, but I think they knew. I know how my kids feel without them verbalizing their appreciation. There is an unspoken feeling of warmth and love that I get from my children, just by being in their presence.

Gerry was truly a mountain of a man. You could feel it in his presence. If you stood next to him, it was like being in the shadow of a big mountain. He was a very accomplished man, both in his job and in the community. It would be a shorter list to list the community programs that he wasn't a part of. He worked tirelessly on the Special Olympics, Red Cross, school board, and the Lighthouse for the Blind. You name it, and if he wasn't on their board, he was at least involved at some level. When I was in public with him and he was recognized, I felt honored to be with him, to stand in his shadow. He took his armor off the day he retired and revealed the softer side that we all knew he had. His picture would be found under compassion in the dictionary, if they would let me put it there. I loved him deeply and miss him so. I almost told him about my abuse one morning while on the patio of his vacation place in Florida. Sue and her mom were out for a walk, and it was just the two of us. I started by taking a deep breath and … and then someone came and took him to the office. So, there I sat, my courage melting away. Maybe, God had interrupted me because I should keep my secret? After that, I never got the nerve up to approach him again. Looking back, both Sue and her mom say he would have been there for me. I worried that he might think me dirty, contaminated, and not worthy of staying with his daughter, my love, Sue. Very soon after that day, he had a heart attack, then cancer in his left lung, then cancer in his brain, and there was no good time to bother him with my secret. It would have been too selfish to speak of this to him.

One day, early on with his brain cancer, he sat at my kitchen table while Sue was downstairs in her beauty shop doing her mom's hair. I could see that he wasn't well. He had been the most voracious reader I had ever met. He had never been without a book nearby. He was like a sponge, absorbing so many things. He was without a book that day. He confessed to me his memory problems, although I could see that without his telling me. He would start a sentence and not be able to finish it, then chuckle and smile. He would ask me to forgive him for forgetting what he was going to say to me. This mountain of a man was weakening, but he still exuded a strength that I wish I had. Even as sick as he was, he towered over everyone else. I stepped in and did what I could, what he would let me do. His cancer left him, but his heart failed him and he eventually died.

My mother-in-law was crushed. They had been together for over fifty years. I helped her with the arrangements and began to go through his desk for paperwork that needed to be completed. He was an accomplished accountant and the vice president of the Niagara Mohawk Power Corporation. As I sifted through the piles of papers on his office floor, sitting in his chair, touching the papers he had touched earlier, I felt him near me, guiding me, and thanking me. His filing system was perfect—perfect until about eighteen months prior to his death. Then, the filing of everything became random. He had suffered in silence for quite a while. I did my best to help, and still do, for my mother-in-law's sake. She is an amazing woman and is always the first to ask, "What can I do?" She always thinks of others before herself. I truly loved my father-in-law and still do. I see him in my head, enjoying my kids and my grandchildren. He passed, still a mountain of a man, and he exists in my head today. *You were my dad too, even though we're only related by my marriage to your daughter.*

My dad, while not accomplished in the community as my father-in-law was, also was a big man in my eyes. Even though I was physically taller than he, I still looked up to him and wished I could be half the man that he didn't know he was. My dad was a land surveyor and had his own practice on nights and weekends. I worked those nights and weekends with him for almost thirty-five years. He was proud of his craft and an expert at it. I sought to follow in his footsteps. I went to college and studied for the career and got the experience so I could take the sixteen-hour exam and get my own surveyor's license. Alas, I fell short of passing the test twice. Only by a few points. But, after the second time, I never tried again. I know I disappointed my dad in this, as he had willed his equipment to me. When his age had advanced to the point where he could no longer work outside, I did some of the fieldwork for him, and he did the maps at home. I can remember sitting in his chair at his desk and feeling like I was somehow absorbing his talent. He was also an accomplished carpenter. He would build anything, for anyone. Nobody knows this, but when we were out surveying, I would stand purposely in his shadow and feel a connection from it, just being able to stand there in his shadow. Being named after my dad is one of the most special things I could have.

I kept my secret past the time my dad died, and I wonder how he would have taken it. Because my dad was Methodist and my mom Catholic, what would have happened to their relationship if I had told him? It certainly would have driven a wedge between them. I know that he loved me deeply, even though I cannot remember even one time that he verbalized it to me. I pale in comparison to either of my dads, and I wanted so much to be looked upon by them as worthy of being a son and a son-in-law.

In stark contrast to my actual "fathers," in the sense that I have stated, Mom wanted me to stand in Neary's shadow, unaware of the pure evil that he represented.

As I carve the hole that my life occupies, I only wish that I am able to fill it with light, in the same way that my dads did so well. I ponder this every day and still look toward the heavens often, asking for help from my two fathers. Do they hear me? I love them both so.

13

DEAR MOM

Dear Mom, are you there? Hello, hello?

I don't think that God loves me anymore. Do you still love me? Will you love me even if God doesn't? I am only twelve years old now, Mom. I am so confused and hurt. I've lived over two years with the terrible things that Father Neary has made me do in God's name. I will tell you, yes, right now. No, I can't. He is God's person on Earth, and he will see to it that God takes you and Dad from me if I tell.

I remember the last time he raped me. He told me he was done with me, and that God wasn't happy with me, as I had displeased God by not being good enough. What should I do? What can I do? I don't want to go on not being loved by God and you, Mom. I pray faithfully every day and try to do my best. What have I done? If I kill myself, I will go to Hell, but if I'm going there anyway for not pleasing God, I might as well end it now and be done with it.

I am cleaning myself up, for the last time, as I hear Father Neary tell you that I will never be a priest. That I don't have it in me. What is it I lack? I did everything he said, no matter how it hurt, and I offered my suffering to the souls in purgatory, as directed. I know God suffered on the cross for me and died for my sins. I just can't figure out what I didn't do. I hear him apologize for my weakness.

This is so hard, Mom. He had told me that he had hair down there because he was a man of God, and when I got hair down there, I would be on my way to becoming a priest like him. I, too, would have to counsel young boys like myself to become priests. I, too, would have to do the things he did to me to other young boys. When I noticed that I was getting hair down there, I was excited, I almost couldn't wait to show Father Neary that I was on my way to becoming a priest! I had tiny hairs growing down there.

Father Neary, though, on this, his last, visit, was angry that I had started hair down there. He said how awful and sick I was. How God could no longer love me. I would forever be cast out of God's love. I was not worthy of being a priest. He said how much I had disappointed him and God, and how you will be let down. I heard him say that he did all he could, but he was sorry, but I just wasn't priest material. I could hear him telling you through the vent in the upstairs door, as I silently sat there, waiting for him to leave. I was never to come downstairs while he was still down there. I was to pray for forgiveness until he had left. I was to pray to be better in God's eyes. I was not to let God down.

Today, though, I didn't pray. I sat by the vent, listening as he spoke. Tears run down my cheeks, and they drip onto the stairs below me. I must not cry, I must not cry! After all, my suffering was nothing compared to God's suffering and dying on the cross for me. Suck it up, as he told me. Don't be a disappointment to God.

I am so sorry, Mom; I just don't know what to do. As I hear the door close, I wait until I hear his car drive away. Then, and only then, can I come downstairs. Maybe if I can find a way to be better, I could go to another priest and start over. I need God's love, Mom. I need your love too.

As I open the door slowly and turn to the kitchen, I see you, Mom. I can sense the disappointment in your expression. I can see the tears in your eyes as you look at me. *Please, God, help me. I don't know what to do. I don't know what to say.* Mom, I am really sorry. With tear-filled eyes, you tell me that Father Neary says I will never be a priest. You tell me that maybe my younger brother has what it takes to be a priest. You tell me how hurt you are and how much hope you had for me. After all, I have been a couple of years in "counseling" with Father Neary.

How can I make it up to you, Mom? I know how sad you are by the look on your face and the tears you rub away. Look at me, Mom. Can you not see the pain in my face, in my eyes? Please look, really look. I hurt too. After all, I had not only let God down, but I have let you down too. I will go back up to my room and pray for help. I cannot make eye contact with you, Mom. I see how hurt you are.

I slowly walk up the stairs, back to my room, and kneel by my bed. I look up at Jesus on the cross and pray for help and for something to make my mom love me, even though I am no longer priest material. I feel the effects from today's "counseling" session. I feel a warm trickle run down my leg. I hurried too much to get downstairs and hear what Father Neary would tell you, Mom. I need to go back into the bathroom and wait for the bleeding to stop. *I am sorry, God; I can't pray to you in the bathroom. I will pray when I come out.*

Mom, as I sit here, I wonder why you never seem concerned about all the time I spend in the bathroom. Why is that? I notice how short a time everyone else spends in here, way less than I do. I wait and wait, until the drips stop. I am no longer bleeding. I use so much toilet paper and tissues, though.

It is stopped now, and I will go back and pray to God. *Dear God, please forgive me for being less than you wanted me to be and unworthy of your love. I am really sorry, but please have my mom still love me. I don't want to live without love. Please guide me. If I follow through with crucifying myself, will you let me into Heaven, and will my mom love me then?* Stop crying, stop crying! God is mad enough at me already.

It is like Father Neary said; I am weak, dirty, and unworthy of love by God or anyone else. I disgust everyone, and if anyone happens to be nice to me, it will only be an act, he told me. I was not lovable. People would see that. Anyone I meet will see through me and know that I am worthless.

I sit at my desk, writing my suicide note. Dear Mom and Dad, I am so sorry to be such a disappointment. I know that God doesn't love me, and that I will be in Hell for all time, as Father Neary told me. But not having your love, too, hurts deep into my soul. I hurt right down to my bones. I have tried so very hard to be good, to be worthy of love, but I have failed. You will find me up in the far corner of the woods in the backyard, on the cross I have made for myself. I have figured out how to nail my feet and one hand, but not both hands, so one hand will be in a sling of rope. Please do not be sad, as I have already been such a disappointment to God and you. Maybe Father Neary is right. Maybe my younger brother will be the family priest you want, Mom. If I do this, maybe, just maybe, you and God will love me. If not, I will be burning in Hell, where I belong. I wish there were some way to fix all this. Sorry. Love, Charles.

As I look at the note, I feel the tears coming back. Stop crying! Stop crying. I must hide this and go race back to the bathroom. Father Neary was very rough this last time. He hurt me extra bad. He was not the least bit gentle, but I know I deserve to be punished. He said so. I am trash in God's eyes, he said. No not trash. He said "garbage," that was what he said, that I am garbage in God's eyes. I really am worthless. Why should I go on? There is nothing for me, now or ever. He made that clear. The one and only way that God might have let me into Heaven was to do what he did and die on the cross. It seems my only way out. Could I really do it, though? I guess so. After all, God did it. I have no thorns, though, to put around my head, and no one to put a sword into my side. Would it still work?

Ow, I feel a cramp, then more blood, and lots of it. It hurts so bad. Hey, maybe this is my way out. Can I make myself bleed to death? Right here, right now? How much blood would it take? Can I squeeze and make more blood come out? If I can bleed to death right here, my pain would be over. I would not have to see the disappointment in my mom's eyes ever again. Come on, bleed more! No, it is stopping. I will have to go back to my original plan, on my desk.

I read it over and over. I am getting mad. Really mad, but why? Where is the anger coming from? I know. I should kill Neary, and then myself. He hurt me, and that is wrong. Maybe God wants me to do this first? Then kill myself. How did I think of this? *Was that you God who gave me this idea? Do you love me? Can you hear me?*

I must plan. How do I do this? How do I get him to come back? If I could, I would sneak a big knife from the kitchen and hide it, and when he raped me, I could turn around and stab him. Yes! That's it. Turn around and stab him, stab him really hard. How many times do I stab him, though? How many will it take? Will he see the knife and grab it from me and stab me? What do I do then? That would surely make me go to Hell for all eternity. After all, I will have broken the commandment "thou shalt not kill." I would surely go to Hell for killing a priest and then killing myself. It would be worth it. I know it would. Other boys would not be hurt by him. This can't be your will, God, to suffer this way to become a priest. It feels so wrong, and it feels wrong to have to pray for forgiveness after each of his visits.

I crumple up the note and throw it into the trash. Later, I realized that it was one of a hundred or more notes, almost all the very same. I couldn't kill myself I was too weak, too scared, too dirty. Even suicide would not be good enough for me. I must remain silent. Save my family from the embarrassment and shame I have. This must be my cross to bear, as I have heard adults tell each other. Someone always has a cross to bear.

I go back down to see Mom in the kitchen. She looks at me and then away. I could still see that her eyes were red. What do I do? Is there something I can say or do to make this all go away? I tell Mom that Father Neary was right, that I don't have what it takes, but maybe my younger brother does. She still faces the other way, preparing the night's dinner.

Mom, can you look at me? Really look at me? Look deeply into my eyes. Will you hug me? Will you love me? Can't you hear my silent screams? I am lost. I fear God, as taught in my catechism classes. I can think of no reason to go on. Is there any?

14

"MY TIME ON THE CROSS"

✦

(original title of the book)

There I was, my pants crumpled down around my ankles. Bent over my bed, I am trying to steady myself under his weight bearing down on me, tears falling from my cheeks onto my neatly made bed, which was now getting wrinkled and damp. It is hard to balance myself. I try and grip the bedspread harder. I feel his sweat dripping onto my back, I smell him, and I hear him begin to moan. I am going to throw up. I glance upward and see his reflection in the mirror mounted on the wall by my bed. There he is, in his full priestly garb, collar and all. I catch a glimpse of his face, as he grimaces while reaching what I would find out later was his climax. As I glance back down to my bedspread, I linger for a moment on the crucifix mounted over my bed. I am ten years old.

As a man turning fifty-four later this month, I reflect. To this day, there are times when I have pain as if the abuse had happened yesterday and not decades ago. You cannot make this pain happen or stop it from happening, no more than you can regulate your heartbeat by just telling it to go faster or slower. It is completely out of your control. At times, it feels like the abuse just happened only moments ago. My rational mind tells me that's impossible, of course, but there are parts of our psyche that we don't control, and they say it did just happen. Our minds, our brains, are still a mystery to us and to the ones who care for our medical needs. Doctors will be the first to admit that they don't fully understand the workings of our brains.

My first meeting with the bishop was the toughest. I was very early on in my journey toward healing. My wife, Sue, had seen him prior to our meeting, to feel him out on the subject of clergy abuse, specifically, the abuse by Rev. Thomas Neary. At first, the bishop played his cards close to his chest and deferred many questions to his victim assistance coordinator. He slowly came around and admitted that Sue was not the first to come in about Father Neary. There had been others, but he left it at that.

Neary had died in September of 2001, and this was now 2002. They wanted to know what Sue was looking for. She told about the sexual abuse that I had suffered years ago. She told them that I was getting some professional help from a psychologist, and that my medical insurance covered so little of it. The bishop agreed to help pay my counseling. The stage was set for me to come meet the bishop and the victim assistance coordinator.

It took a bit of coaxing, but I agreed to meet with them, as long as Sue could come too. If there really are angels, guardian angels, then God has sent me Sue. She somehow can read me, even without a single word being verbalized. She is my protector from further damage, and she is more supportive than you can imagine.

The four of us met, and it went better than I expected. I hadn't been sure that I could be that close in person to another "man of God." I was weary, shaking, and quite frankly, scared. What would they tell me? What would I ask? I made notes, so that I could remember the main points I wished to cover.

I told them that, above all else, I felt the need to mend the gap between myself and God. I want things to be right in my relationship with a God who I felt abandoned me when I was a child. As I said earlier, after the physical sexual abuse, after the mental and emotional sexual abuse, and after the spiritual abuse, I find I can't turn to God. Rape is wrong in any shape or form. That being said, if a person is raped by another person, then they should be able to turn to their faith for help. If your sexual abuser is a man of the cloth, your faith resource on Earth, where can you turn? Faith is where we each should be able to turn, and do turn, in times of need. When a loved one passes, or any other relative or friend passes, we almost always say that we will pray for them. If you feel you are too dirty, too tainted by the sexual abuse you have suffered at the hands of God's representative on Earth, where do you go? Inward. That has been the only place I could turn to—inward. You all have heard the armchair quarterbacking where it is suggested that we stuff it down and repress our feelings.

The "faithful" who tell you how you should feel and act only tear at the emotional scars and scabs you have suffered. They don't seem to get it how your faith is tattered and mostly gone. They tell you to pray. Sure, I prayed. I prayed hard, just maybe, I prayed harder than they ever had. However, when you are ten and spend hours on your knees, at home, in church, alone in the woods, where you look around and try to feel closer to God, and you pray for this sexual abuse to end and there is no answer from God—then you wonder what possible good there can be from praying. You think, why weren't my prayers answered? Why was this allowed to happen from the fall of 1961 through the spring of 1963? I'll tell you, because I walked in those shoes and I am an expert, not by choice, but I am. You feel dirty, shameful, and abused by your God too. You have the lowest self-worth, and you believe that even God doesn't love you.

The meeting went on for about ninety minutes or so. I expressed the need to come back again, alone, without Sue. The bishop had said that he would act as "Neary" for me to yell at, to swear at, or whatever. A date was set. When I confirmed my appointment, I told the bishop it was to be me and him only, no one else. He wanted the coordinator there, but I said no, just the two of us.

We spoke frankly. We agreed that some of what we said would forever be just between us and never leave his office. If nothing else, I am a man of my word and would not retell the sensitive things he wanted to keep just between us. It was not unlike the seal of confession he told me. He had told me that he had some past success with the victim confronting the abuser. He said that there was some healing accomplished. Father Neary was dead, though, and I could not confront him in person. The bishop said to pretend that he was Neary and talk to him, yell at him, no-holds-barred, let it all out. Sounds good on paper? Sounds good in theory? I started three times to unload on the bishop, but I failed. He wasn't Neary; he wasn't the one I needed to unload on. Part of me felt that I should continue anyway, but it wasn't to be. The bishop then went on to tell me to visit Neary's grave site and yell at him there. He mapped out where Neary was buried and how to get there. After a while, I did just that. I stood over his headstone, gazing down on it. I felt nothing other than I was glad he was dead and had to stand before God for his religious and felony crimes committed. He may have escaped this Earth without prosecution, but I don't think he could slip past God.

I instead detailed what Neary had done to me. I didn't pretty it up at all, and I spoke very frankly to the bishop. My story was the first he had heard in a first person account with this level of detail. He was visibly moved, his hands shook, and he teared up as the details unfolded before him. I spoke of looking up at the crucifix over the head of my bed and thinking of God's suffering on the cross. It was then that the bishop gave me the original title to my book.

I asked where was God for me in my time of trial? The bishop replied, "Charles, that was your time on the cross. You looked up, and that was you on the crucifix at that moment. God knows how you suffered. When Neary was doing this to you, you were on the cross then." Hence, my original book title *My Time on the Cross*.

I asked for some Bible passages to read to try to close the gap I felt between myself and God. A little humor ensued, as he went to his floor-to-ceiling, wall-to-wall bookcase, but he couldn't find a Bible in his office. He left and got one from another office, and we read passages. On my next visit, he had two Bibles in his office, one he signed and gave it to me. Sadly, I still feel a loss, a gap, a void, between myself and God. The more I read, the more I look, the more questions I come to, instead of the answers I had hoped for. Sad, truly sad.

Something bothers me, though. While meeting with the bishop, I asked him if he believed Neary was in Hell or not. He said that we can't sit in judgment of another. The "judge not lest ye be judged" line was used. OK, I'll give a little. However, in today's paper there is an article about a nun who is being considered for sainthood consideration. A group of local nuns are headed to Hawaii to dig up the body and bring it back to Syracuse, New York, where it will be stored. Tell me something, how can a person be selected for sainthood without being "judged" that they are worthy of becoming a saint? Certainly, judgment was used to check out and verify this nun's worthiness for sainthood. So, judgment can only be used when the outcome is in favor of the Catholic Church? Can they "have it both ways?"

Aren't any of you mortified at the thought that they are digging up a corpse, and then trying to verify it as that of "Mother Cope?" Once verified, they plan to transport this long-dead body here to "enshrine" what's left of the body of someone who lived in the 1800s? It's creepy to think about digging and moving her long dead corpse. If the Catholic Church wishes to judge her worthy of sainthood, do the actual remains have to be dug up? Is this just a ploy to distract us from the ongoing sexual abuse of children by priests? Where did God say it was up to a man to declare another a saint? How about leaving that up to God and not playing God?

How can sainthood be given and then modified? Wasn't St. Christopher declared a saint after being judged worthy, only to have it "revised"? St. Christopher has been removed from the Universal Calendar of Saints based on a lack of historical evidence pertaining to the details of his life. The Bishop said, "We can't speak ill of another." Someone had to speak ill of him to have his sainthood taken away? He had to be "judged" unworthy, after already being "judged" worthy?

Does a double standard about standing in judgment come to your mind too? Isn't that a little like playing God? Aren't we all mortals and shouldn't we leave it up to God to decide who is a saint or not? This truly confuses me. Is he a saint? Is he not a saint now? What does it really mean to be removed from the Universal Calendar of Saints?

I changed the title of this book to *In the Shadow of the Cross* because I did not want to give anyone the impression that I somehow equated myself to Jesus. I never did, or ever would, compare myself to Jesus. Since the bishop, himself, made the analogy to me being on the cross, I thought it proper to use it as my book title. After hearing from some of my Catholic friends that had read my manuscript, I reconsidered a change to the title I would use. They all told me that they were offended by my comparing myself to Christ by saying I was on the cross. That was never my intention to equate myself to Jesus in any way, shape, or form. Even at Christ's crucifixion there were two others being crucified at the same time. I felt this analogy was OK, especially since many died this way. Thus the change in the title to *In the Shadow of the Cross.*

I empathically state that I do not equate myself with Jesus. While the bishop made the analogy originally, I felt it not proper—thus, the new title.

15

CHOICES

Someone once said, "A person who lives on hope dies of starvation."

Life is full of choices. We all make choices each and every day. While we are tied to playing the hand we are dealt, we still control which card to play and when. You play out the hand you're dealt at birth, as your life unfolds before you. There are no discard or draw cards allowed. Accept it. Don't waste your time here on Earth trying to alter your hand. It is what it is.

Each and every day, we choose when to get up so we can arrive at work on time or take the kids to the bus stop or directly to school, etc. We choose whether to drive the speed limit or not. Life, simply put, is an endless list of choices we make—when to play what card—until our days here are over.

When someone tells you that they have no choice, then they have not explored all the options or they have chose to do nothing. We must live by our choices; after all, we are the ones who made them.

There are things that are beyond our control. Bad, very bad things. But there are good things out of our control too. We all, at some level, know right from wrong, good from bad. We choose which to do. However, the very hardest things you will do in your life are also the hardest choices to make. Doing right is hard. It is so easy to stray off the path. It is easier to let someone else do something rather than extend ourselves. Why? Great question. One of many I wrestle with myself.

It would be easy to sit back and ignore the sexual abuse being performed against young boys and girls by priests. However, to stand up for those children shouldn't be as hard as it is. Our children are the single most important aspect of our lives. They are paramount to our futures. They deserve nothing less than our complete protection from evil. Harm comes to everyone, but evil preys upon children. Always listen to your children, but more importantly, listen to what they don't say. Look into their eyes. Peer into them. Children are sponges for knowledge; lead them and love them.

It hurts when some priest says that he was abused as a child and therefore he couldn't help abusing children himself. Oh yes, and the world is flat too. That evil being, that horrific priest, knows right from wrong. Don't buy into that load of crap. That is the lamest excuse we have ever heard. It sickens me to see a sense of forgiveness toward those priests, or to hear people say that it wasn't his fault because he was abused. Those forgiving people have been "blinded by faith"; they do not possess "blind faith." There is a difference, and it's a big one.

My life's journey has taken me to many places. I met a woman who had overheard the topic of clergy abuse being discussed by me to another. She asked if she could tell me something. Sure, I like to hear others and their views. She had been in the mental health field for over thirty-five years. Her unit was the place where men who sexually abuse children are kept. They were locked away, not enjoying a nice pension, health benefits, nice home and car, like many alleged priests are. She said that there are men there who had been there for decades, as well as recent patients. Some have been chemically castrated by use of medications, and others have been physically castrated. She can say, without exception, that these men continue to have urges and strong sexual drives. Neither method stops these evil men from wanting to have sex with little boys and girls.

This brings me back to choices. They know what they do is wrong; they will tell you if you ask them. But given the chance, they would do it again. Choices. Those of you who say they are "sick"—you are dead wrong. What they do is "sickening," but they are not sick. Cancer is a sickness, not the premeditated rape of a child. Those who rape don't have a disease, but rather a compulsion. There is a huge difference there.

Face it, we all have impulses. Some of them may be wrong, and we therefore don't go there. Knowing right from wrong is black and white; there is no gray area when it comes to children.

Choices. What happened to me and countless others was a result of choice by our abusers. The priest first befriended me, then my mom and my family. A conscious choice was made by him over the span of a few months, all the while knowing it was wrong, but he didn't care. It was against the very things we were being taught in catechism class. It was not a senseless random act of onetime violence on a person; it was well planned and carefully laid out, and all the time his eyes were on the "prize." Yes, the prize, me. I was the prize that he chose. Looking back at some of the faces he made at me, which burned into my little ten-year-old brain, I recall the face he made the day he "took" me. I could swear that he was salivating as he looked down at me from his tall, adult body.

Choices, choices. He could have chosen right and not wrong, but he chose to act out his compulsion and damn the word of God he preached. He got his prize, and I lost my innocence. My childhood was brought to a screeching halt. Gone, forever and ever. My view on life was forever changed. I became the fringe child—the one always on the outside, not really a part of my peers.

Wallow in self-pity? No, that too is wrong, without exception. The three hundred or so survivors/victims I have met to date do not want sympathy or pity. If anything, we want empathy. There is a big difference. We want a sense of justice and atonement, but most of all, we want accountability. The Catholic Church should say that what happened to us is a felony crime, shameful to the Church. While it is a sin, it is firstly a felony crime. Then use the Church rule on sin if you want, but, first and foremost, it is the willful commission of a felony. Pick up any paper, read any news story, or watch television on this topic, and you will see that it is handled in the public sector as a felony crime. The right choice is being made in the public sector, where sexual abuse is not hidden as if only a sin has been committed.

Choices, choices. Happiness is the feeling of being happy, enjoyment, soaking in the good. God has placed happiness here on Earth for us. I believe that being happy does not happen; rather, it is also a conscious choice. If you sit back and wait for happiness, you will be gravely disappointed. It won't come to you. You must make the choice to seek it out and embrace it, ever so tenderly, so softly. Life may seem bleak at times. I feel that, from time to time. This is where family comes in and also God's creations: a warm summer breeze, feeling the warmth from the sun, hearing birds in song, even a crisp fall day as the many colored leaves make their dance to the ground around you. The silent magic of snow falling gently, making a beautiful white blanket, just so pure and perfect. The smell of the air right after a thunderstorm, the cleansing effect of rain, the show of lightning flashing in the sky. Choose to embrace these things, and you will be on the path to happiness.

Choose to overlook the little faults in your spouse, children, and grandchildren. Cherish the unbridled love that a child shows his or her parent and the unconditional love from a grandchild. Lose yourself in your spouse, as he or she surrounds you with an embrace, and you melt into the other person. You can almost physically feel the love penetrate your being; your spouse is there for you. If only that feeling could be bottled up and stored for use on demand, as you needed it. There really is no better pick-me-up, and words are not even needed. Your loved one only needs to be there, and it happens. How cool would that be if you could bottle this and place it in the cupboard? Then, when you were feeling beaten down by everything, you could run to that cupboard, fling open the door, grab that container, open it up, and drink from it or pour it over your head? Choose happiness, and it will work more often than not. I know that my wife, Sue, is the center of my Earth, the very center of my being. She makes the choice that she will be there for me, no matter what. She offers total unconditional love and support. When I fall, she has made the choice to be there, whatever it takes. She feels that God had a hand in bringing us together. Hug your children and embrace your grandchildren; there is nothing better than that. You can see their purity and their souls as you look into their eyes and beyond.

I made the choice growing up that the underdog would not suffer if I were around. I didn't have to even know the victim. Bullies would not corner a peer and start in on them if I was within earshot. I chose to put myself physically between bullies and their prey. It was a choice I made. I knew that nothing the bullies could do to me could be worse than what had already happened to me starting at age ten.

Choices drive us all, whether we wish to admit it or not. The act of doing nothing is a choice. We do, however, know right from wrong, especially when it comes to children. That is what it is really about—the choice to save and protect our children from this kind of evil. The saying "been there, done that" applies to me, I feel, except in my case it is "been there, suffered from that."

Make the right choices. You will know them, as they are the hardest ones to make and do. Choosing to do nothing and to not get involved is a wrong choice.

16

GET PROFESSIONAL HELP!

If you have been the victim of sexual abuse by clergy as a child, or at any age, there is one thing of paramount importance: get professional help! If I were to list the single, most important thing to do, it would be get professional help. If you are a victim, and take nothing else away from this book, please seek the help of a professional.

I feel that I hit the jackpot with my doctor. He is Stephen Driscoll, PhD, a New York state licensed psychologist. It is rare to hit one over the fence the first time, but I was fortunate. The more victims/survivors I meet, the more I know how hard it has been for some of them to find and retain the kind of help they truly need. Tragically, some have also been abused by their therapists. That is an unconscionable act. Being on the "inside," being both a childhood sexual abuse victim and an adult survivor, it sickens me every time I hear of a case of re-abuse, especially when the abuse comes from a professional. When that occurs, the victims tell me that they have no more options. They may have been cast out by their families with cries of "no, not our priest! How could you even accuse him?" This is the case more times than I want to say. The victim, rejected by his or her family, cannot even turn to their faith, as it was their spiritual leader, their priest, who ravaged them in the ugliest ways you can imagine, and then some.

Without the support of family or faith, the two most primary areas of support, you feel truly alone. Very much alone. This only hurts you further and adds to your feelings of being unworthy. It is tough enough when your family accepts and believes you. It's very tough when you disclose your abuse to them and you sense they doubt you. After telling some family members, you can read the terror in their eyes for what you went through, but others give you a doubting look. Talk about feeling dirty. Being asked how much money it would take to satisfy you hurts so bad. To be asked to convert hundreds of violations to me as a child into a monetary figure smacks of prostitution. "X" number of dollars for each act of anal intercourse, "Y" number of dollars for each oral sex performed on the priest, and "Z" number of dollars for all the other forms of sexual abuse I suffered. Being re-abused by your own sibling—how nice.

While on the topic though, name me a more deserving group of people to be financially compensated. I have a tough time coming up with one. To say there has been no financial impact on any victim is equal to saying nothing really happened. In my own case, I was told by my high school counselor that I was not smart enough to attend a four-year college. I wanted a shot, I wanted to try, and if I failed, I failed. Back in 1969 though, at my high school, you could not get into any college without a recommendation from your guidance counselor. He didn't even try to sugarcoat it. He flat-out told me that I would fail. I lacked the confidence to push long enough and hard enough for it. The scars of abuse follow you everywhere you go, at every turn you make, simply everywhere. While you don't dwell on it, you have no control over when it takes form in front of you, triggered by many things outside of your control.

Compensation? One of the most deserving groups is survivors who have no one, or those who cannot manage adequately, financially. There are expenses, medical conditions, and surgeries in some cases, and there is work time lost. Some survivors are unable to keep a job. Survivors deserve help with therapy costs, reimbursement for lost wages, and compensation for pain and suffering caused by priests. Just because I look good on the exterior doesn't mean that I haven't become a master of disguise, a master of stuffing my emotional well-being ever deeper with each passing day. My doctor aided me with that insight tremendously.

Who knows what I could have become if my view of self had not been tainted by Neary? Emotional rape far outreaches the physical. The physical side may heal and leave scars, but the nonphysical self can be damaged beyond repair. Many victims have difficulty uncovering their hurt and anger and confronting these negative and painful feelings.

As I said earlier, I struck gold with Dr. Driscoll, who was the very first doctor I saw when I was ready to get professional help. However, arriving at the first appointment, I became that ten-year-old boy with his silent screaming and desire to run away. Luckily, my ever loving, ever present wife, Sue, held my trembling hand, slowly drawing me to the door and inside his office.

Sue first said that I should seek professional help only days after I disclosed my abuse to her. We made an appointment with my primary care doctor, but instead we saw a trusted member of the staff upon arriving. The "plan" was to talk of the pain I live with day to day from the deterioration of my spine. By this point, I had had two lower back surgeries and one neck surgery. The operations were little more than a Band-Aid than a cure. My spine continues to deteriorate. In the fall of 2003, I had yet another neck surgery. Two titanium rods and screws hold the vertebrae in place. The pain goes on, but we'll get to that later.

The woman we saw at my primary care doctor's office is a gem herself. Shortly after my request that she recommend a professional to talk to about my physical pain, Sue said something like, "Tell her the real reason." Immediate panic set in, and I felt like the proverbial deer in the headlights. Sue opened the door, and I gave in to tell the doctor's assistant of what happened, in as brief a manner as I could. She only had one name on her list, Dr. Driscoll, whom she felt was right for me. An appointment with him was made.

When we left home that morning to see Dr. Driscoll, I told Sue that we were going to "feel him out" before disclosing my abuse. I would start by talking to him of the daily pain I was in from the continued deterioration of my spine and the emotional toll of being told that the deterioration would take my life some day. I had already gone the pain management route and was taking upwards of twenty-five pills a day. I stopped the numerous medications after a short time, as the side effects were extreme. All I felt was dopey and still in pain. They recommended I consider a morphine drip administered via an implant tied to the problem areas of my spine. I had had morphine in the hospital after my last surgery and didn't like the effects. I told him that I was looking to address the pain management and pending mortality.

Shortly into this, my first session, Sue had already sized him up and somehow knew he was it. He was the doctor who would help her husband. Woman's intuition? I believe so. This woman was sent to me via something bigger than either of us. During a brief pause, Sue interjected with the real reason we were there. She just came out and said that I was sexually abused by a priest as a little boy. The next few seconds felt like hours, with panic, immediate sweating, and shaking. What had Sue done? We had talked about this before coming to the doctor and had agreed on what was to be said on the first visit. If I felt comfortable, then at a future visit, if all was going well, I would tell him of the sexual abuse at the hands of Rev. Neary.

I looked at Sue, then at the doctor, then to Sue and back, and it felt like hours were passing in those few seconds somehow. I felt like I had been laid out, fully exposed. What to do now? What to say? I tried to whisper to Sue about our ground rules, and she smiled back, saying this is the doctor for you. I just know it. Pretty lucky I am, being married to such a smart woman. But at that instant, I had my doubts. I felt the release of tears coming, and there was no way to stop them; they were like a runaway train, each tear a train car, loaded with all my hurt pouring forth. How did I feel? Good? Bad? Hurt? Exposed? Faint? Awful? I felt all of these and more at the same instant. I never felt that that could happen. Sue had betrayed me, but somehow, it was OK. I needed that nudge to begin my path toward healing. She knew that he was the right doctor, and he had the skills necessary to help. I'm married to one of the smartest women ever. I still tell her that she deserves better than someone with all these health problems and someone with this secret that was now out. What could she possibly see in me that I don't?

The first visit came to an end only moments after it started, I felt, but at the same time, it seemed like hours had passed. I know of no other way to state it. I did, though, feel lighter, somehow, upon getting up and walking to the car with Sue. How could the disclosure of my sexual abuse at such a young age by a priest give me the physical feeling of being lighter? There is so much that I didn't know and still don't. Sue's judgment was right on target. Dr. Driscoll was the one. The therapy began.

In the followings weeks, I began to tell him of the abuse I suffered, both the physical and nonphysical. A more caring doctor does not exist. He walked me down the trail of my abuse and medical conditions. First, we talked in detail of my physical ailments with only some talk of my abuse on each visit. Dr. Driscoll somehow knew the proper blend of topics and ever so gently guided me. There were many tearful sessions, some with Sue at my side, some alone with the doctor. I saw him weekly, and time passed. Each departure left me feeling lighter somehow. Too bad it wasn't my weight going down!

Dr. Driscoll explained how I handled the abuse at age ten and gave me the tools to help in the suppression of the physical pain I now felt. Funny how some things tie together when you feel they can't be related. As Neary continued in his sexual abuse of me, I developed a mental place I would go to. He could take my body, but my mind was mine and mine alone, unreachable by his violations of my little boy's body. I became a little numb at his arrival and adopted the attitude to just withdraw and not resist anymore, to let him do his thing, and, that way, it would be over faster. It worked. He did his thing and I withdrew to a safe place in my mind, and then it would be over. He seemed to know that I had given in, but he never let it show, and he was still having the time of his life, back there, behind me, as I was transported elsewhere. My mind was mine, all mine.

I used to feel that if I took this to my grave, if I kept my dirty secret, then it would be for the best. I felt that if I told anyone about it, then Rev. Neary had won on the last front, because my mind was the only place he couldn't violate. God knows he used all the physical places to violate me.

This, wrongly, leads to so much deep guilt. Why had I not stopped him? Why had I let this go on? Why had I become numb to it? Did he think that I liked it after I stopped my physical struggles against a full-grown man? Why didn't I feel anything as he raped me? I would feel the effects, the rocking and swaying of his body, the groans of joy he was experiencing, the sweaty smell, and his vile breath. Was I then a bad person? Was there anyway back to save myself? Where would I go? Where would I turn? I only found answers to these questions after some forty-plus years of wrestling with them, with the help of Dr. Driscoll.

Did God put Sue and Dr. Driscoll in my life's path? If so, why? God was nowhere to be seen or felt as I prayed my little heart out as a little boy. Why would he do it now? Had I suffered enough that he finally felt the need to help me? After all, many years were spent in my Catholic upbringing learning that God had suffered and we must offer up our suffering to him and bear our cross.

Bit by bit, Dr. Driscoll helped me to peel away the layers of protection I had built up over the years. The process was not that unlike the peeling of an onion, which also makes us cry. It has been a painful journey, and I don't know when it will end, when I can say, "OK, it's over." Maybe never. Maybe sooner than I know. I recently told Dr. Driscoll that I feel the beginnings of feeling OK, that this is the right path. However, I look over my shoulder for the next thing to come at me. Feelings like this, I have heard others talk about, but never have I felt this way. It is scary, uncharted territory, and maybe I shouldn't be here. Is this what others feel when they are happy? At peace with themselves?

He asked me how I dealt with the physical pain from my spinal problems. I told him I would have a conversation with myself. I would say in my mind, *stop it; there are other people out there in more pain than you are, so just cut it out!* That seemed to work best. I was, after all, a master of stuffing my feelings. The story comes to mind about how a man felt bad about having no shoes until he met a man with no feet. I forced myself down that path.

I always felt that if only I could take this all to my grave, it would be for the best. No one in my family would be hurt by the knowledge—not my parents, wife, children, or grandchildren. The grandchildren don't know and will only be told if and when their parents decide it to be. My line in the sand stops with my children. As I said earlier, by keeping my dirty big secret, I had final control. I owned it, because my mind was the one place Neary could not get to. If I somehow came forth with what he had done to me, he would have won the final front—the only place I felt I could keep pristine, untouched by him.

As we jointly peeled away at the layers, Dr. Driscoll kept me from blaming myself. I feared that it had been my fault, as I had taken no definitive course to avoid it. This was the adult in his early fifties imposing what the ten-year-old should have done. I ever so slowly unburdened myself and laid my emotions out, still holding back, as I wasn't yet convinced that what I was now doing was indeed correct.

Dr. Driscoll spoke of how retaining the feelings within my inner being could be likened to emotional food poisoning. I had never looked at it that way. He said that when you ingest bad food into your body, your body doesn't just sit there. It reacts to help itself. You either vomit up or void the poisons you ingested. Your body removes what shouldn't be there. He likened my abuse along the same lines. In order to feel better, no, be better, I needed to empty my emotional vault. It was like a vault. All tightly kept away, out of reach from everyone but me. I held the only key, and now I had given Dr. Driscoll his own key to the vault. I openly and completely trusted him. Trust is a huge issue with victims such as myself. Dr. Driscoll and Sue can both tell you that I trust very few people and only after empirical data have accumulated to the point that I feel safe. It is a very short list, as they both can tell you.

As I let it out, layer by layer, Dr. Driscoll helped with the bumps and valleys. He knew just how much to draw out of me and how much I could handle. He is such an expert in his profession. He told me that the guilt I was feeling was not guilt, but regret. Guilt is a good thing. It is a mechanism by which we shouldn't make the same mistake twice. If you do something questionable, then the next chance you get to do it, guilt should stop you. I had no guilt. I had regrets, many regrets, but no guilt. It took some convincing, but he prevailed. There was always a nagging in my head, that if only I had had the guts to kill Neary myself, it would have stopped him from harming others, but that was not to be as a small boy. It does hurt that, maybe, just maybe, if I had carried out one of my many plans to kill him and myself that I could have saved the victims younger than I. As victims come forward from almost all the churches where he served—and some are twenty-five plus years my junior—I feel that they would have been spared, if only I hadn't chickened out as a boy. Therein lies the answer; I was a little boy, a ten-year-old boy. Other victims of Neary were as young as six.

I feel that letting this out in all its details to the doctor does aid in the healing process. I don't know how or why it does, but it does. I do feel an unburdening of sorts. I still cannot walk down this path without Dr. Driscoll. He picks me up when I stumble or try to retreat in the reverse direction. Regret, not guilt. Regret that it happened to me, no guilt for it happening. A tough one to swallow whole, but broken down, it works.

The shame, embarrassment, feeling of low self-worth, and scores of "labels" we give ourselves are not fitting. I am beginning to see how I had no control over the situation. He was a big, adult man, and I was a little boy.

Memories, memories. Can't stop them because you never know what will trigger one. If only you knew all the triggers, maybe you could steer clear of them? Not likely, because a trigger can be as simple as a color, or a breeze, or pipe smoke, or smoke at all. The doctor and I are working our way down my list of vivid memories to try and ease the pain they still cause. I say to those who comment to forget about it, come back to me once you have been raped and then you have the right to tell me how I should feel. It's just one more tug on the scars we will always have.

For the most painful of memories, Dr. Driscoll uses a technique called EMDR (Eye Movement Desensitization and Reprocessing). He has used it to help veterans with their wartime memories. Why does it work? I can't say. It somehow fools your mind into a change of feelings about an event, and the pain is lessened. It is a method that is related to hypnosis where the patient is walked through the traumatic event with detail, and this process replaces the pain with distraction. All I know is that it works very well on my deepest pains. You can never erase an event in past. It isn't like a chalkboard that can be erased of all traces as if it never existed. An event can, however, cause you lesser pain if EMDR is successful. Going into it, Dr. Driscoll told me that it might not work, but I pressed on to try it. Now, as some of the events burned into my brain pop up by themselves, maybe by a trigger I didn't even catch, the associated pain is less, or it is gone entirely. It's like you can't un-ring a bell but you can lessen the effect of the noise it caused when it was rung. Sort of like standing next to the bell as opposed to being a block from it when it is rung. When a mental image comes forth, Dr. Driscoll suggested that I consciously add myself as an adult to intervene between Neary and my child self. Strange as it may sound, it can and does work, almost every time. I told you—my doctor is great.

There is something that I refer to as collateral damage. My wife, children, mother, mother-in-law, and siblings, are also all "victims" of Neary's sexual abuse of me. It ripped at my very being to tell them, but at the same time, I found out that my secret wasn't completely secret. There were moments between the tears when we shared some kind of recognition of past events and how I reacted to them. What wasn't apparent to me was apparent to them. Things of the past fell into place, they would say. "That's why you did such-and-such." "We wondered where you were coming from and why you felt the way you did. I guess it wasn't as complete a secret as I thought it was.

I see the doctor as often as we feel I should, which is once a week, most of the time, but on occasion, every two weeks. He gives me the tools necessary to help myself. He guides me, rather that leads me. I thought my healing would be more like a cookbook—here are the ingredients, now go bake that cake. I couldn't be further from the truth. There are days when I come home and weep, and there are days when I come home with a smile on my face. Both of which, I am convinced are necessary in my healing. Neary didn't win by my disclosing his raping of me. It wasn't a sign of weakness to tell what happened to me. I feel guilt no longer, only regret. The other emotions are coming around too. How much further do I need to go? I'm not sure, but there is comfort in the fact that I am in the hands of expert guides, both in the doctor's office and at home with Sue.

Dr. Driscoll said to me recently that talking to me and reading the chapters I have written so far have given him the "password" into my world. While I am not his first sex abuse patient, I am the first patient who was sexually abused by a priest. After reading my first chapter, "Dear God," Dr. Driscoll said it hit him in the chest like a mortar shell. Then it would let him back, only to be drawn in again. He has said it is a very powerful chapter, to see it through the eyes of the ten-year-old I once was. To this day, this very moment, I cannot talk to God without yelling at him; however, I also believe that God knows and doesn't mind.

I told the doctor recently that the more I read and know about abuse, not only mine, the more I find that I don't know. Make sense? I just find a sea of information out there and within myself, and I learn more each and every day. The imaginary horizon that I established at the beginning of this journey moves further away, the closer I think I get to it. Do you really think the world is round?

17

"COME OUT, COME OUT, WHEREVER YOU ARE"

It is a little like "hide-and-seek" when we reflect on being sexually abused by a priest. They toyed with us. It was a twisted game they played. We were their prey, or reward, or treat. These people, these evil beings dressed in priestly garb, are not men of God. They deserve no respect, no reverence, and no tolerance.

The Catholic Church has stated they will no longer request gag orders of litigation as a means of agreeing to a settlement between the Church and the victim. Pardon me while I stop to hold my sides as I laugh. This might better be known as splitting hairs. I recently went to court on behalf of a "Jane Doe" case. Her lawyer was there, and the accused priest was there with two attorneys, one from the diocese and the other one, a private attorney. The allegedly abusive priest was asking for, you guessed it, a gag order. When taken to task on it, the Church's lawyer said that the Church was not asking for the gag order, but rather the private attorney retained by the priest was asking for the gag order. Splitting hairs? You bet!

We must come forward and expose these priests. Until we make them known, the clerical abuse continues. I am willing to bet that some or many of you holding this book right now have been sexually abused or know of a family member who has been abused.

We were victims, and now that we are adults, we should also call ourselves survivors. As little ones we were victimized, but we grew to adulthood, and now we are survivors. I tell my support group that. The worst, the actual abuse, has passed; we have made it to adulthood.

It takes time—a lot of time. It is now forty-four years since my abuse started. Time heals all wounds? Baloney. The abuse has left permanent scars on us, scars deep into our souls. Many, including myself, struggle with our ties to God and the Church. *God, where were you?* Sound familiar?

We need to come forward, to tell our accounts of the abuse we suffered. Remaining silent keeps our children and grandchildren at risk. It is too late for us who are now adults, but we must save the young.

I kept it inside for forty-two years. It ate away at my insides. It affected my physical and emotional well-being on all fronts. Many of you know how it feels. We need you to come forward and disclose what happened to you, not only to expose this evil for what it is, but also to begin your journey toward healing yourself.

I too hid, as I said, but I wish dearly that I hadn't. The priest who raped me had a career of over forty years of abusing children. It's hard when I meet a person younger than I who suffered from his abuse. We need you to stand up and speak.

My doctor could tell you that I carried guilt around for too long. We are not guilty of anything. This was done *to* us. Neary was an adult, and I was a child, just like many of you.

I would be remiss if I didn't talk about the stigma of disclosure. Yes, there are people, even family, who will look down on you after you tell them, as if you had any say in the matter as a child. We were kids, *kids*. Replace your feelings of guilt and shame with feelings of regret. We have nothing to feel guilty about. My predator is dead, and he can harm no more.

If your perpetrator is still alive, no matter where he is, you can bet that he is still abusing children. They don't stop; they don't quit abusing just because they were removed from priestly duties or even defrocked. As long as they breathe, they still harm. Our local paper recently ran a story from another city where a ninety-four-year-old man pleaded guilty to a reduced sentence of eight years for the sexual abuse of five young girls. These men don't stop.

We can no longer wait for the Church to do the right thing; the Church has proven itself to be faithful to the priests, not the parishioners. The churches have names of known and suspected rapists, but they keep silent about their names. What happened to "do what Jesus would do"? If you read the Bible, you can see that God not only would be sickened by these acts, but God believes in the death penalty for it (remember Matthew 18:1-6). By hiding these names, isn't that the same as coming up to someone and saying, "I know that one of your relatives, a member of your family, sexually abuses young boys and girls, but I'm not telling you who." Just whom do you not trust your children with? Is the abuser an aunt, uncle, parent, grandparent, brother, sister, cousin, niece, or nephew? Just whom can you trust your little ones to be with, and whom can't you trust?

Should we expect more from the Church? Of course. They are supposed to be our spiritual leaders, our source of strength for faith, something to look up to, especially in times of trial.

Doing the right thing. That is what it's all about. It is not easy, but that only serves to prove it is worth it. If you have been victimized, please disclose the abuse to your loved ones and the authorities. Visit the SNAP Web site at www. snapnetwork.org or look for a local support group in your area. Come to us, we will help. E-mail me directly if you want, at charleyb@highstream.net. Sincere help is out there.

18

INTRODUCTION TO SEX

Intro to *sex*?

Think back about your introduction to sex. Looking back, I have a picture in my mind of "normal" sex. First, I must give you my definition of normal sex. To me it is between a man and a woman. I believe that man was created with an appendage and woman was created with a place for that appendage. I also believe that what adults do outside of this definition is up to them. I will not sit in judgment of two adults doing consensual forms of sex among themselves. The key word here is *adults*, meaning that both people are over the age of eighteen, just as the law defines it. With that definition in mind, let me expand on this topic.

Ideally, introduction to sex happens between a man and woman or a boy and a girl, with their respective ages being equal in category. If one of the partners has crossed the age boundary lines clearly stated by law, then I don't approve of that kind of introduction to sex.

Teenage years are a prime time for equal-age exploration of sexuality. While many of us were taught from a young age to save ourselves for marriage, life happens before that time. My slant on this is shaded by my introduction to sex. In my mind, it should happen as a result of deep caring, love, and affection between two people. A natural attraction—as I will lay out for you.

Think of your own first experience. Was it a tender kiss or an especially warm hug? The gentle exploring of one another, "petting," as it might be called? The pure and simple exploring of the opposite sex as you feel a bond being created? Pleasure for *both* partners as you develop an intimate relationship? A sense of emotional happiness? A closeness that you feel only the two of you could possibly experience? Warm, loving, and caring?

Maybe I'm way off base as I approach this topic, as my introduction was not defined by any of the above. Something to also bear in mind is that it was the fall of 1961 when I first experienced sex, at age ten, and it was with a Catholic priest. Today, the teenage generation is more "savvy" than teenagers back in 1961 were.

Back then, there were no music videos, questionable song lyrics, and sexually explicit movies and television shows. Back then, we had only three TV stations, and they signed off each night and were not on again until morning. Even the shows on TV were bland, compared to today's shows. Those of you who remember *Ozzie and Harriet* or *The Donna Reed Show* or *Leave It to Beaver* or any other show of that era must remember how those happily married couples slept in separate beds. They were married couples, and yet we never saw them share the same bed.

Without getting up on my soapbox, I want to say that today is very different. Pick up almost any magazine, newspaper, or watch TV or movies, and you'll know what I'm talking about. Once again, I will not sit in judgment of what our children are seeing, reading, or watching. No, on second thought, I will sit in judgment. I think a happy medium should be achieved between 1961 standards and today. Don't hide behind the First Amendment just to show questionable media. I really don't think that our forefathers would approve of the way their Constitution has been twisted today to permit the things it allows. There, I said it. Now, I'll get down from my soapbox.

The teenagers of today know way more than I knew back in 1961 about sex. In this vein, maybe they are "smarter" than I was and maybe they know intrinsically what the line is and when to draw it. Back then, even the word sex was not in our vocabulary. *Gone with the Wind* was banned from our Catholic view because it contained the word "damn" in it. The Church established their ratings and decided what movies were acceptable for us. They made the decisions.

It would be so nice to be able to look back fondly on my first sexual experience. As I said before, I have a mental picture of what I wanted the first experience to be. I wanted a warm, loving, and caring experience between a girl and myself—not forced anal intercourse with a Catholic priest.

At ten, I knew nothing of sex except how to spell it. My first encounter with Rev. Neary was what I learned much later was French kissing. That man of the cloth was pressing his big adult mouth over my small, virgin mouth and forcing his tongue down my throat so violently that I had a gag reflex. What was that? I was clueless, as were my peers, I feel. I was told that that was the beginning of my path down the road toward someday being a priest. Father Neary had the worst teeth I had ever seen. They were yellow, and he had bad breath, smoky, from his ever present pipe. His eyes would, at times, look all black, like a shark's; it looked like there was no white around his irises. He would seem to my little ten-year-old person as an ever growing giant, getting bigger by the second. I would swear that he had more than two arms, as he pulled me ever so closer, and at the same time he would rub me "down there," on the outside of my pants.

What a wonderful experience it could have been if only it had occurred between a girl and me. No one should be introduced to French kissing the way I was—no one should experience what followed the kiss, either. At age ten, back in 1961, no kids were kissing, much less French kissing. At least in my circle of friends. Girls still had "cooties," and we didn't want to get them, even though "cooties" were never defined. All we knew was that we didn't want them.

Intercourse. I'm not sure if we knew what it meant, much less what it was. We would giggle among ourselves when someone would say it, not letting each other know that we truly didn't know what we were laughing about.

Rev. Neary, looming over me, as he penetrated my little ten-year-old anus. Hot, sweaty, heavy, priest bearing down on me as I tried to steady myself. He barked out orders as we "offered up my suffering for the souls in purgatory," or to God himself.

Looking back, instead of this image, I want to see a "normal" loss of virginity. Between a girl and myself, not this. That is just one more thing forever lost, forever corrupted, by this Catholic priest. You see, it is *way* more than just the physical act. It goes way beyond that. Think of yourself as if you were born wearing rose colored glasses. This is the way you should see and experience your childhood, through rose colored glasses. Then imagine that one day, at age ten, you are violated sexually by a trusted Catholic priest. A family friend as well as a spiritual leader. You are dragged down a one-way path. Forever changed. Your view of life is shattered and your rose colored glasses are forever broken. You now see life through plain glasses. You see the stark reality of true life—evil, manifested by your spiritual leader, your moral compass. Everything from that moment on is no longer the same. Everything you say and do for the rest of your days on Earth is viewed from a different angle. You see things differently from those who got to live out their childhoods and make gradual, normal transitions to adulthood. Unless you are an adult survivor of this type of child abuse, it may be a far reach for you to grasp our point of view. My innocent, young life was destroyed forever by Neary's evil. I am searching, ever searching, for answers, explanations, and a feeling of worth. I am worth something, aren't I? After the abuse started, I no longer laughed with my peers, not like they would laugh. I knew evil that they couldn't even imagine. I had to insulate myself from my friends so as to not cause them harm. They must never know. Even as an adult, wearing dark tinted glasses to alter my view of the world, I still see clearly what others don't even know exists or are afraid to admit is there. There aren't glasses tinted dark enough to block out what I see clearly, day in and day out.

Was your first sexual intercourse between yourself and a member of the opposite sex a willing culmination of your love, caring, and feelings for each other? I hope most of you answered that yes. What does that feel like? Am I a hopeless romantic, on some level thinking that your first sexual experience was as I wish mine had been? Mine was filled with terror for me in all aspects, as you can probably discern from my writing. A pleasurable introduction to sex is one of the scores of memories that I will never have.

I had a life-changing event, which some of you either will not or cannot comprehend, any more than I can wax fondly of my introduction to sex. From that fall day in 1961 at age ten, I was forever changed. We have to play the hand we are dealt. There are no draw cards, and there are no cards to be cast aside—there is only the one hand you're dealt. To this day, I look at my hand, and, in addition to asking *why this hand*, I try to best play out what I've been dealt. It is too late to prevent what happened to me, but there are new children born every day. Maybe, just maybe, I can play my cards in such a way as to save some others from this terror.

As I advanced from age ten to twelve, when the abuse stopped, I became more worldly. I, too, became curious about girls, once the "cootie" stage passed. I also began, with my friends, to call each other "homo" or "fag" or other terms. But I don't believe any one of them knew what those terms truly meant. They were only used to poke fun at boys who goofed up playing sports or who lacked athletic ability, or those who simply tripped or fell down. There was no malice assigned to those words as there is today. It meant no more than calling them "boogerheads" or "mommy's little boy." They were washed away almost as they were being said, by saying "no, you are" or the like. However, as time progressed, I learned that what happened to me starting at age ten was a homosexual experience; it was "sex." I had had no idea that it was sex. Was this the sex we joked about as early teens? Or was it something altogether different? I had no clue. I tried to go along with my peers, but I never knew for sure what was being said.

Then the day came when I knew what the acts were, and that they were not something to make me priestly. It was in seventh grade. It was my first time in the boy's locker room. All of us were naked at some point between changing into our gym clothes and showering before getting dressed for classes. Rev. Neary had told me that pubic hair (which I only learned the name of at this same time) was only for those of us who were to become priests. However, he stopped seeing me at the first signs of genital hair, which also led me to more confusion. It began to settle in as I saw that all my peers had more or less pubic hair—that may have been the first concrete thing that caused me to fear that Neary had been lying. The pubic hair was supposed to mean that I was on track; however, all my peers were also getting hair, and they couldn't all be becoming priests. Or could they? I was so confused. As I tried to sort this all out, I remembered my early Catholic teachings at Holy Family School in third and fourth grade. Before we started each day, we would pray. The end of each morning's prayer was for all of those who were not Catholic, because they were doomed to Hell unless we could save them by bringing them into our faith.

While not a rocket scientist, I could put together that all my non-Catholic peers were getting pubic hair too, and they sure weren't on the path to Catholic priesthood. It is hard to put into words, but I then developed a feeling that my world was growing somehow smaller—not expanding like I expected it do with knowledge. The more I wrestled with my thoughts and feelings, the more my world shrank. Here I saw many naked boys but felt absolutely nothing exciting about it. But I was a homosexual, wasn't I? After all, that's what they do, don't they? I would look around the room and feel no attraction to any of them. But aren't homosexuals supposed to like boys and not girls? In the early 1960s, there was nowhere to turn. I couldn't tell my parents, as I still felt, on some level, that there was a chance Father Neary could have them taken from me. This I could not gamble with, and I was already over my neck in confusion. There were no counselors at school, save academic advisors, to whom I could turn. My siblings? No way. Could they also be taken from me? Would they understand at all? I could only turn inward, to wrestle with all my thoughts alone.

As time progressed, I found myself strongly attracted to girls. I found strange feelings overcome me at times in the presence of a girl. What was this? I had already had a homosexual "affair," but I felt no feelings toward other boys, only toward girls. Was this normal? Being attracted to girls? I remember that the girls were released from class to attend a special girls-only class, but what was that about? What were they told? Why wasn't there a class for only boys? Another thing—why were girls allowed to go to the bathroom any time they asked, but us boys were told to wait until after class? What was that about? If you have to go, you have to go, don't you? Only girls can go? Yet another question.

One day in my early teens, I was taking the short walk home from my friend's house when someone threw a magazine out the window, almost at me, it seemed. I stopped, picked it up, and there it was—a "girlie" magazine with naked women in it. It was tame by today's standards. It showed only side or back views, or legs crossed, but there were breasts. Lots of them. Page after page. I felt that strange feeling again, with something stirring "down there." This was attraction to the opposite sex in spades. But, how could this be? Wasn't I supposed to be a "homo," as my friends would joke about? It was clear that that was not the case. I was clearly drawn to the opposite sex. Then what was this relationship I had with Father Neary about? It was sex, but bad sex. I immediately felt disgusted by my very existence. I stopped and threw up on the side of the road. What had I been part of from the fall of 1961 through the spring of 1963, from age ten to twelve?

That was the real beginning of my downward spiral about my low self-worth and my feelings of truly being dirty, filthy garbage. How had I let that happen to me? Was Neary's path my real choice, or had I experienced real evil in the flesh? That question, I would not struggle with until years later.

How to hide the magazine? How to sneak it into the house without it being detected? I first hid it outside, under some rocks near my house. I could not take any longer to look at it because Mom knew how long it took me to get home for dinner, and I was and still am a poor liar to this day. She would surely not believe any story I made up on the spot. How could she be so good at lie detection and yet still be so oblivious to my silent screams when I was being sexually abused by Neary? I place a lot of importance on eye contact, and to this day, I look people straight in the eye, and if they look away, I question what they are saying. I would make direct eye contact with my mom back then, but she didn't see my suffering, or couldn't see it. Which was it? I hope it was the latter.

I did find a way to get the magazine into the house, and I hid it safely, only to have it be found by my mom while she was cleaning. All she said to me was that it was filthy and disgusting and that my dad would need to talk to me. Once again, I felt pushed down yet another path that I didn't want to walk. Was it truly dirty and bad to like females? Was Neary right after all that all females are bad and dirty, and to be avoided?

My dad had the "talk" with me. Looking back, his delivery was almost humorous. My dad, ever the engineer, told me the following: "Charles, your mother has told me that it's time to tell you about the birds and the bees. Your penis can become hard like your index finger." He showed me his outstretched forefinger. I had already found this out. "A woman," he continued, "has a special place on her body where you insert your penis and fluid comes out, and she is then pregnant. Don't do this until you get married." That was it. Short, concise, to the point, as if that were all there was to it. What about feelings, emotions, and anything else that was also involved in this sex? The talk was over. It was done. Dad had had the "talk" with me. So that was it? That talk only brought up more questions in my mind.

As an aside to this subject, it's interesting that when my mom was first told of what had happened to me, she initially blamed my dad. She said that it was his fault for not telling me during the birds and bees talk. Once again, I was floored. Not part of the birds and bees talk? What? What? I was ten. The abuse occurred years before the "talk." I then told her how Sue and I had decided when I should talk with our boys. We had decided that we would somehow know the right time, and we did. However, it was the birds and bees talk, not an adult-man-to-little-boy talk about sex between the two. That would never have come up. I told my mom that that topic never crossed my mind to tell my boys. The "talk" was to be about the natural attraction between men and women, and the physical and emotional side of that, along with STDs, and the responsibility that maturity would bring to them. The deviant behavior of a Catholic priest never entered the "talk," nor would it today, unless I felt it appropriate. Learning of your body's capabilities is tough enough without adding to it such behavior as I had experienced.

I have been intimate with only two women in my life, both of whom I married. The first marriage was very brief, as it wasn't meant to be. My first wife is credited with "saving" me, as my current wife now tells me. Sue has said she is actually glad I had the experience of my first marriage. It helped me walk down the path I am on today. Sue and I have been married over thirty-four years and have four children and eight grandchildren so far.

The period from age ten to adulthood was forever ripped from me, and I only have my ideas of how it could have been and how it should have been. While I do not dwell in the past, it is forever there. It happened, and no words can change that. It will never be forgotten, although maybe the pain associated with it can fade over time. I am worth it.

The complete safety of our children should be paramount in all our lives. Take no chances with yours and listen to what they don't say. That's right; listen to what they don't say.

As you reflect on your first sexual experience, remember how it felt. Cherish it, savor it, and give thanks. You had what I wanted.

19

RELATIONSHIP DEVELOPMENT WITH THE OPPOSITE SEX

As I begin this chapter, I have reservations about how to write it. By all means, it is not the hardest chapter to write, but in some ways it is so hard. You wouldn't think, at my age, that the little boy I once was could still surface. I will be writing about relationships that happened long before I even met my wife, Sue. I love Sue and want so much not to hurt her. I want so much to hold back some of my feelings, but like Sue and everyone else who truly loves me says, it needs to be written with true feelings and emotions. It is so very important that the average person really understands the great tragedy of my story, and that can only happen when I dig into the past. I need you to understand how being raped at any age, let alone age ten, will impact every part of a victim's life.

I found my first real attraction to one girl in particular in junior high school. We began by writing notes and passing them to each other in the halls. We didn't share any of the same classes at that time. I couldn't believe that someone was interested in me. My experience to date had been that any girl I spoke to rejected me, unlike my male friends whom girls seemed to like. What was it about me? Did they know? How could they have known? But this girl seemed to like me "as is," and she had cute, dark brown hair that flipped up about her shoulders. She had a warm smile. She was very smart and got better grades than anyone else I knew. School seemed so easy for her, and I had to put much more effort into my studies than she did.

Once school broke for summer, we corresponded by regular mail about once a week on average. She was home most of the summer, and I was at my parents' camp. The letters made me feel that there was someone outside of my family who liked me. We moved from pen pals to more, as our school years advanced. We went "steady" during high school, but we had our breakups too. Our parents thought that we were too serious, so they stepped in from time to time.

When we were broken up by our parents, we felt horrible. We tried to see each other anyway, but her mom had "spies" in the school who would rat us out. We couldn't even speak to each other in school, much less on the phone. During some of these times, my friends would try to fix me up with girls they knew. Some of them were fun, and we had small boy-girl parties with parents always present.

A few of these girls wanted more than kissing, and I too felt that I wanted more, but didn't know what. What more? Some guided my hands under their blouse, while there was a look out for the ever present parents in the next room. Others wanted my hands actually under their bras. I liked it, but was equally confused by it. I know how good it felt, and they seemed to like it too, but was this it? Was there to be more? I was terrified of the more. The more I knew was not where I wanted to go, if it was what Neary had done to me. Back then, you must realize that even *Playboy* only showed breasts and nothing more. What was "down there" on a girl was a mystery to me. None of us boys knew, but they all bragged like they did.

By senior year in high school, our parents felt that my first "steady" girlfriend and I were old enough to handle our relationship, as we had never stopped trying to get back together. On the day following the prom, we went on the after-prom picnic. While there, we had intercourse, and it was the first time for either of us. We were excited, and I was also scared and not really sure that what happened was what was supposed to happen. It wasn't like with Neary; it didn't hurt either one of us.

Later, we became engaged, went off to college, and got married. It wasn't to be, though, and we parted ways after a short time. She wanted college and a career, and I wanted a family.

20

INCREASED SUPPORT FROM UNEXPECTED PLACES

Yes, I received genuine support from places I did not expect. After our local newspaper put my name out there, and after I testified before the Senate hearing on the sexual abuse of children, I was out there, exposed. OK, if they are going to mention the victim's name (in this case, me) and not the name of the priest, even using "alleged" in front of his name, then hold on, here I come! After that day, where I was named publicly and not the priest, a wonderful local newpaper reporter did the research, and interviews, and got Neary's name out there in the paper. I was incredibly grateful for this and fellow victims of the priest started calling me, and asking for help and some just to thank me for having the courage to go public. The paper will not print the name of an abuser without credible evidence.

Since that spring day in 2003 when I first testified, I have been open and vocal in my community. I have had newspaper articles and editorials written by me, and there have been some written about me. The local media, TV, and radio now seek me out to ask my opinion about how the Catholic Church handles the priest abuse issue and how the Church affects an adult survivor of childhood sexual abuse by a "Holy Roman Catholic Priest." They all now know that I am very candid, and that I see things from a different angle from most people. I used to have to seek out the media. But only two days ago, one of the local TV stations was here to ask my view of an accused Episcopal priest. I have been interviewed on several topics since, some have included the Vatican's position on clergy sex abuse along with my take on the Pope's stance on the crisis, some have been about certain cardinals, bishops, and priests, to name a few.

Not long ago, there was a message left on my machine by a person saying he was FBI and he wanted to meet me. He left his name and a cell phone number to call back. I thought cell phone? What about an office number? Was this a serious call? Or was I being set up? First, I called the FBI 800 number to ask if this person was indeed a real FBI Agent. They verified that he was a real agent.

I called the cell phone number, and, after a brief talk, a meeting date and time were set at my home. The agent wanted to know what I know about the sexual abuse of children by priests. I told him, even though I had verified his identity, that I would require seeing proof of his identity before allowing him to enter my home. He was impressed at my diligence. Before the agent arrived, he asked if he could bring another agent with him—an agent attached to the attorney general's office. I agreed, but I told them that I would need to see the other person's ID in addition to his. That was not a problem.

They showed up on time, and after verifying their IDs, I let them in. We sat at my kitchen table for most of the afternoon, as I detailed what we had found out about the abuses. The details sickened them both, and we gave them copies of related items and information that we had come across. We still keep in touch and track the ground we have covered. I cannot identify the agents or exactly what has been discussed, at least not until it comes to fruition.

There is a certain respect gained between myself and the bishop over the last few years. The meetings with the bishop have been about my healing with God, and how I see changes that must be made in order to protect all children. The bishop gave me his residential telephone number, which only his staff and family members know he told me. While I have not called him at home yet, the door is still open to calling him. I consider it a sign of great respect that he gave me the number, not worrying if I would put it out there for all to know. When he publicly speaks about the sexual abuse and I take exception to what he has said, I never personalize it. I take exception to the verbiage and not the man. It is never a personal attack on the bishop when I speak, only on what he and his staff have said, if I feel they need a response. On some level, I feel that the bishop now knows what these priests have done to us. We have had a life sentence placed on us by these evildoers. I believe that I was one of the first to actually give details, holding back nothing, as I told him of what Father Neary had done to me. As I mentioned before, the bishop was visibly shaken as my account unfolded before him, and he became teary-eyed and shaky. He apologized on behalf of Neary and his fellow priests and the Church. I can't say for sure, but I feel that sometimes the bishop has only heard filtered accounts of abuse because the diocese lawyers and church staff under him have not told him everything.

A short time ago, the phone rang, and the man identifying himself as our local district attorney wanted me to come in to discuss clergy abuse. He said that the local victim assistance coordinator for the diocese had said that we should meet and talk. Sue and I headed off to his office. In the beginning, a little small talk ensued to try and diffuse the tension in the air. I found out that the DA and I were the same age. He said that he and his family were Catholic, but that he would not allow that to interfere with the law. Sue and I gave him some information on abuses that we felt should be looked at and reviewed. It was professional and businesslike. Another newfound respect was being forged. I would go home and send him what documents I felt were pertinent.

I then read him my "Dear God" chapter. During the reading he looked at me intently, while his assistant seemed to squirm in his seat as I spoke. It was obvious that the DA was moved by what he was hearing. After I finished, he said that my account needed to be out there, that it was very powerful and could he have a copy to use. I respectfully declined, but told him that when my book was published, I would give him a copy. He restated how this needs to be read by everyone.

The DA looked over toward the corner where his TV was and pointed at it. He said, "Charles, if that were a time machine and not a TV, I would travel back in time and stop the abuse you were going through." That one sentence spoke volumes of support to me. The DA said that he had never heard about sexual abuse from the angle that I had presented. We all know that there is no such thing as a time machine, but if there were, he would have helped me. That gave me a good feeling, and I will carry that moment with me forever.

As we got up to leave, he came around his desk and hugged both Sue and me. He gave me his business card, and on the back were his cell phone number and his home phone number too. Trust—he trusted me, and I trusted him. We will work together toward protecting all children from that kind of harm.

21

DENVER: SNAP

Denver, June 2004

The three-day national conference of SNAP (Survivors Network of those Abused by Priests) was held in Denver in 2004. Friday was to be a leadership training day. Saturday and Sunday were open to all leaders and victims/survivors.

Sue, I and a fellow leader were fortunate to have a sponsor to help defray some of our costs. Another adult survivor had paid for our airfare and conference fees. Meals and accommodations were self-paid.

We arrived on Thursday morning and took the shuttle to the hotel. Our luggage was unloaded, and I paid the driver. However, I was already getting nervous of what to expect, and both Sue and I noticed. I feared the unknown, and I was also afraid of actually meeting with many of the people who belong to the national group of SNAP, like Barbara Blaine, the founder of SNAP from Chicago, David Clohessy, our national director, and Father Tom Doyle, to mention only a few. Some of the authors of books that I either owned or wanted to own were also at the conference. I had corresponded with both Barbara and David via e-mail and telephone, but I was about to meet them face-to-face. I was to meet Barbara for the first time, but I had met David at the lobby day when I testified before the Senate hearing. I was excited and scared at the same time, which distracted me enough, that I set my glasses on the back bumper of the shuttle van. You guessed it; the driver took off with my glasses on his rear bumper. Then what? Unconsciously, I had packed the other pair with my expired prescription in my luggage. I had never done that before. It was as if my subconscious knew something that I didn't.

The hotel staff did their best to find them. Sue walked several blocks, looking on both sides of the street. The hotel staff called the shuttle company, who radioed the van, but the glasses were not on the back bumper by the time the driver stopped and checked. I would have to just wear my old ones. What had made me bring an old pair? Who knows?

Off to a banner start, and I needed to eat, as my blood sugar had dropped. I knew without having to test it. We ate lunch in the hotel and looked around for the others who were arriving Thursday. Many came Thursday, as the leadership training was to start first thing on Friday morning. Throughout the day, we met many people—victims/survivors, others who support us, and speakers for the conference. The conference was well organized, and we knew who was who from their name tags, which were color coded to show who was a presenter, a local SNAP leader, a Denver SNAP member, a national SNAP member, or just a general conference attendee.

Thursday night, it was tough getting to sleep. We were anxious and excited about what lay ahead. Friday came, and we were addressed by our national leaders. We broke up into several work groups, to come up with a strategy for our mission and what we wanted for the future. We arrived at very impressive results, suggesting the direction we should go and the steps to get there.

Saturday all were present. There were several hundred by this time in our meeting room. One by one, they told us their heart-wrenching stories. They also described how they were developing their coping skills. They too said, as I have said, that the most important thing is to seek professional help, in addition to attending local SNAP chapter support group meetings.

After a group session, we selected from the small breakout sessions, which ran concurrently. Most sessions had more than one time to attend, to enable us to attend almost all the ones of interest.

A common thread was unfolding in both the main meetings we attended and the breakout sessions. As an adult survivor, I identify from a different level with other survivors than nonvictims do; I identify as the "been there, suffered from that" listener, if you will. Even though it was such a heart-wrenching day, there was a common thread that surfaced. I was amazed, shocked, and sickened by what I heard throughout the day, over and over, by many victims' stories. I can think of no one with whom I didn't recognize a common thread. These monsters, these evil priests, used the same words and methods on all of us. With each session, I would find something that sent a cold chill down my spine. It amazed and frightened me that the actual words used on me, to rape me, were the same as the words used on so many others from all over the United States. You would think that all these priests either were educated in how to concur and rape us, or they met privately with each other to compare notes and develop their plan of attack on us. The pattern was so much the same, with the same words, that you would swear it was scripted and disbursed to these priests. Do they secretly have closed-door meetings on how to abuse us? A chilling thought.

Neary's routine of saying the "Our Father" during the rape and making me say it with him, repeating the "thy will be done" over and over, the absolution given me after he "finished," the threats of having God take my parents away, the lectures about offering my suffering up to God, etc., etc., etc. My experience was identical, word-for-word, to that of many others. The exact words during the abuse were not just close, but exactly the same, as if it were some kind of abuse ritual. Ritual abuse is not limited to the religious definition and can include compulsive, abusive behavior performed in an exact series of steps with little variation. How could these similarities occur without the priests taking the same "abuse seminar" together some place, somehow? Was it taught in the seminary? In some dark corner? It goes beyond coincidence—the similarities in deeds and verbiage that these predators use on us. It truly chilled me to the very marrow of my bones. All of you reading this know that if you are married for any length of time, you can usually finish your spouse's sentences, and the spouse can do the same for you. Sue and I have that connection. Almost without exception, this kind of connection also occurred between the victims I spoke with. To have an instant connection with a person you have known for such a short time is mind-blowing. More than once, I got goose bumps, listening to and exchanging accounts of the abuses.

It was hard to get a firm count on how many were at the conference at any given point because it was a three-day event. People would come and go throughout the conference; however, at any given moment, my best guess would be that there were around 300 attendees.

During one of the group sessions we all attended, suicide was discussed. I had no idea how many of us didn't survive our abuse and had taken their own lives. Most took their lives in awful ways, such as standing in front of a train and a myriad of other violent methods, in addition to the gun-in-the-mouth way of ending a tortured life. I reflected on my own thoughts of suicide as a youngster. As I said before, I wrote hundreds of suicide notes, but would reread and discard them in the trash, where I felt I belonged too—in the trash with the rest of the garbage. The sheer number of those lost was discussed. As a footnote, Father Tom Doyle believes, from his twenty-plus years of research on clergy abuse, that only one out of every sixty victims ever comes forward. Bearing that in mind, we had a list of, I believe, 137 known victims of clergy abuse who killed themselves. The number is just that, a number, a statistic. We sat in the group session, looking at each other as we pondered the number of deaths. Then, some of the parents, spouses, or others who had a suicide in their family told their accounts. To demonstrate the magnitude of the event, as names were mentioned, an audience member would come forward, hold a picture of the deceased, and remain on the stage, holding the picture. As it unfolded, I could feel the charged atmosphere in the room. I held a plaque for an unnamed victim, who, even in death, wanted to remain nameless. It was one of the most moving events I have ever seen. To say the number, 137, is one thing, but to see that many people standing shoulder-to-shoulder is a vision that burns into your permanent memory. You can visit the SNAP Web site at www.snapnetwork.org and click on "Denver conference" to see us on stage. It is so powerful that you may weep, as I have done while viewing it. Even more sickening is the idea that these are only the ones that we know about. How many others have taken their lives without anyone knowing why? How many have suffered in silence until they break, no longer able to stand it, and tragically end their lives? Some suffering victims are penning their suicide notes right now, as you read this. This very moment, ending it all is crossing someone's mind. Please take a moment of silence, set this book down on your lap, and bow your head. Close your eyes for a moment and say a silent prayer for them. Ask God to extend a ray of hope to them as he did to me through Sue. Part of all of us dies when a person dies by his or her own hands. It is so sad, so very, very sad.

Barbara Blaine, the founder and president of SNAP, gave another moving lecture. She has devoted her life to helping others, trying to protect others, and trying to reach out to all victims of sexual abuse by clergy. Barbara is an amazing and powerful woman, admired by many for her passion and drive to address sexual abuse by clergy and bring it to the forefront. At one point, Barbara hit a nerve in me that I wasn't aware of yet. She said, "Your neighbors will never knock on your door and tell you thanks. Thanks for trying to protect and keep safe their children. Thanks for all you do to put an end to sexual abuse by clergy so our children may be allowed to be just that, children." Powerful words from Barbara, when you let them sink in. I believe that childhood is a onetime adventure that, once broken by clergy sexual abuse, ends in a mere instant. It is gone forever. From that instant forward, you look at your childhood peers from a different angle, a different place, almost developing an envy of their unbridled excitement at "normal" childhood activities, which you now only enjoy a little. You have lost your connection to them as equals, and you live on the fringe, because they don't know what you know. They don't feel like you feel. You try to piggyback on their fun, but, sadly, you remain on the edge, aware of what is out there. What is out there is stuff that they don't know and you shouldn't know.

As previously mentioned, my biggest goal is to believe that God still loves me after the dirty, foul, vile things that I was forced to do. I really believe that my soul is tainted and unrecoverable, in some sense. When I read the day's list of breakout sessions, one was on spiritual healing. Sue went to another session, as I entered the spiritual healing session.

Once inside and seated, I began to look around for familiar faces from some of the other sessions. My gaze was soon at the front of the room. Remember triggers? Standing there was a woman in the black and white priestly garb, looking back. I froze, and I was not alone. I heard very little of what she was saying initially. I was too distracted, trying to hear her words without zeroing in on the priestly garb. While not Catholic, she identified herself as a priest. I looked toward the door to plan an "escape." However, when I had entered the room, I had walked clear across it to sit near the front in an empty seat. To leave now, she would notice, as I would have to walk right in front of her to get to the door.

I felt trapped and unable to move. I began to sweat and shake. Fear was coming, and I knew it. How could she dress like that in a seminar about abuse? I now began to squirm in my seat; I could not find a comfortable position. Just then, a man sitting on the opposite side of the aisle from me spoke up.

He politely and respectfully asked her how she could wear that priestly garb, knowing that we were victims of sexual abuse by a priest. Her answer was curt. She said that a man in the earlier session had taken her to task on the very same thing. Her reply was that this was her priestly outfit, and if he didn't like it, he could leave, which was the same thing she had told the earlier victim. She went on to say that she needed to wear it. She needed to wear it out in public, as if she could not be "out of uniform," so to speak. This was my chance to leave, but there I sat, frozen in my seat. He told her that other priests were in attendance at the conference, and they were in street clothes, as they were sensitive to the victims. She would not budge, and she passed out a one-page form to survey those in attendance. It was to be filled out at the end and handed in. As much as I tried, I couldn't get past the collar—her words were muffled by the wearing of the black and white.

Needless to say, you know what I wrote on the evaluation paper. Just a short time later, after the breakout sessions were over, as we headed back to the main large conference room, we saw the same priest sitting in a booth, selling her wares in street clothes, yup, in her street clothes, in public, no less. As I passed by, I did a double take. I told Sue that this was the priest who could not be out in public without her collar.

Sunday was the last day of the conference, and the sessions were to end by noon to allow us to travel home in a timely manner. The three-plus days had been a roller coaster of highs and lows—very low lows. I found myself in one of the lows Sunday morning, as we prepared for the closing meetings. I was in the shower. I washed my face and, as I rinsed under the shower, looking down, I began to notice the water as it disappeared down the drain. The shower became my tears. I began to weep uncontrollably. I could feel my tears mingling with the tears from the showerhead. I wept for myself, I wept for the other victims I had met over the last few days, and I wept for those still out there being abused at that very moment. I ran through a medley of emotions as I watched all the "tears" go down the drain. I began to feel dirty, ashamed, guilty, and not worthy. I thought of how the drain took the tears away, down the pipes, into the sewers. The rotting sewers—maybe that's where I belong too. *Let me become my tears, and take me to the sewers to join the other filth.* That's where I truly belonged, down there.

Then I heard Sue call to me. Her radar, her sixth sense had been activated. I had been in the shower too long, she thought. Her voice, her concern for me, woke me up out of my low, and I looked up from the drain, turned off the water, and got out.

I told Sue what had happened and once again, she knew what to say and do. I love her so deeply.

22

SPEAK UP

Since my disclosure a few years back, I have been approached to speak before various groups, both large (several hundred) and small (a dozen or more). I have become the SNAP leader for the Syracuse/Oswego, New York chapter. I also hold support group meetings. I have to credit the Utica area chapter and their leaders for helping to get our chapter off the ground. They were a great help.

One of the largest groups I spoke to was the Call To Action group. They hosted their statewide conference here in Syracuse, New York. Members from Buffalo, Rochester, Syracuse, Utica, and Albany were in attendance. Their format was not unlike our Denver conference. They opened by introducing the panel members who would be speaking, myself among them. After the general overview, there were concurrent sessions in breakout rooms. I sat on a panel and stayed in that room, as the attendees moved from room to room.

On the panel with me was Father Tom Doyle, a Catholic priest. For over twenty years, he has traveled in the United States and eleven foreign countries, educating people about the sexual abuse of children by clergy. He has one of those demeanors that make you feel at ease moments after he speaks. He had spent many years tied to the Vatican and is also a canon lawyer. He had also been a chaplain in the armed forces. He knew from which he spoke. He did not mince words; he called a spade a spade. He spoke to the true evil that the Vatican allows, all the way down to the local priests and parishioners. He said that now is the time to take action, not tomorrow, and not next week. Children are being raped this very moment.

Between one of the sessions, was the media part. Both Father Tom Doyle and I were interviewed on camera. After the media left, he came over to me and said that he felt I would make a difference, a real difference in this movement. Here was this world traveler, a highly educated priest, telling me that I would make a difference. When the next session began, Father Doyle gestured toward me and told the group that I am what the Church fears most. I turn my anger into educating the unknowing public. The Catholic Church doesn't fear the poor soul who leads a broken life because of their abuse. They fear me, because I am not broken or worn down. They fear me because I attend conferences like that one, and I was coming for them—so they'd better get ready.

Father Doyle's praise humbled me; and I stumbled a little as I started to speak, trying to absorb what Father Doyle had said. I had never seen it that way. I saw only that all children should be safe; that not one more child should be hurt. I saw that it was past the time to draw the line in the sand; it was time for proactive help.

There also was a representative from VOTF (Voice of the Faithful), a Catholic group that wants to "keep the faith—change the Church." This is an honorable stand. After all, it is not the faith at fault here. The blame lies with the men who lead the faith: the priests, bishops, cardinals, and the Pope. Yes, even the Pope.

Between sessions, there was about ten to fifteen minutes to get a glass of water or sneak outside for a cigarette. During each break, not one, but each break, people came to me and called me aside to whisper in my ear. They were young and old, men and women. Each told me of their sexual abuse by a priest, and each thanked me because I was doing what they could not do. All of them said that their spouses didn't know, and that they would most likely never disclose the sexual abuse they had suffered from their parish priests and monsignors. Some said that they were passed around like candy, from priest to priest.

This sickens me at the deepest level possible. I gave each a card with my home phone number, e-mail address, and home address. I told each one of them to contact me at any time. I offered to aid them in telling their spouses too. Without fail, I told each and every one to seek professional help, and that I would be available for the rest.

After the final session in late afternoon, a man of slight build stood just beyond arm's reach, as if he wanted to speak to me, but was wavering. I gestured for him to come over, as I gathered my things. He bent over me and said that he was a Jesuit priest and had been one for forty-two years. He asked for my forgiveness for what his fellow priests had done to me, and he made a tearful apology on their behalf. He went on to say that he, in forty-two years as a priest, had never been in the presence of a holier man than I. I was stunned, but before my mind could process what he had said, he dropped to his knees, took my hand, and placed it on his head. He then asked me to bless him and forgive him. I told him that I am not a man of the cloth and am not qualified to bless him. He said, "You are. You don't know how much you help others in pain." He asked again, "Please." I did as he asked and looked up for a bolt of lightning to strike me; after all I was a lay person, not an ordained priest. He asked to hug me after he stood, and I felt something spiritual pass from him to me, and some of my ever present anger began to dissipate. What had just happened? I still reflect on that day from time to time.

The VOTF groups from Syracuse, Cortland, and Rochester have each invited me and my fellow SNAP leaders to come address their meetings. We have traveled to all their cities and have spoken before all their groups. They are, as a group, warm, caring, and truly passionate about God and their faith. The Rochester group, however, was met with some concern as they found it hard to believe my account as it unfolded before them. I feel that some people have a hard time with the truths around us, not only the sexual abuse by priests, but all bad things. I call it chosen ignorance. This modified form of ignorance is found in people who, if confronted with certain truths, realize that they have to accept them and thereby acknowledge evil, and that scares them. Opening up and letting the truth in might knock them off their perceived center. It is too hard, period. The people truly touched in VOTF tell us or send a note of thanks, and for these, we are thankful.

A plain, brown paper-wrapped package came in the mail recently. Upon opening it, I saw that it was a patchwork quilt about four feet by five feet. Many little scraps of cloth, carefully joined by loving hands. Two squares have suggestions of a black cassock and Roman white collar. The maker of the quilt states, "In its variety, I feel it denotes confusion and the world "mixed" up. There are dark spots for the dark times and bright squares, so, hopefully, some good and brightness will come in the future. The other pieces of cloth were of happy times, mothers and children, peaceful settings, happy things." A note inside stated that she felt we were "scraps,"—the "scraps" that the abusive priests treated us like. They would use us as a scrap is used and then simply toss us aside. I was moved to tears. Holding it in my hands, I could almost feel others' pain and suffering, as I touched each panel. It is a magnificent work, worthy of a prize. I was deeply humbled by the receipt of the quilt. This woman got it; she really got it. She has a deeper understanding of what we have gone through. It is rare. I am so thankful for the quilt, and it is displayed in my living room on a quilt rack. It is something that I will treasure for the rest of my days.

How often do we hear from the local diocesan people—the bishop, the communications director, the victim assistance coordinator, and others—that this abuse is not restricted to clergy, but, rather, it is a societal problem? It does occur outside in the public realm. When was the last time you heard of a sex offender not being held accountable for his actions once caught? The Church treated the abuse as a sin only and nothing more. Out in society, sex offenders are not moved to another community quietly. "But protest that priests are 'no worse' than other groups or than men in general is a dire indictment of the profession. It is surprising that this attitude is championed by the Church authorities. Although the extent of the problem will continue to be debated, sexual abuse by Catholic priests is a fact. The reason why priests, publicly dedicated to celibate service, abuse is a question that cries out for explanation. Sexual activity of any adult with a minor is a criminal offense. By virtue of the requirement of celibacy, sexual activity with anyone is proscribed for priests. These factors have been constant and well-known by all Church authorities" (Sipe 227–228).

23

ON THE EDGE

Yes, on the edge, on the fringe. After the abuse ended, I started my life on the edges. I participated in sports. I was on the wrestling team, the lacrosse team, and the flag football team. I took extra classes that weren't required, such as creative writing and calculus. I was in the school plays. I searched and searched, looking for my place among my peers. It was a place that I never found.

In sports, when we were victorious, the team would be enjoying the win. I, too, tried to join the celebration. They were happy, very happy. It was bluntly obvious to me that they were happy on a level that I just couldn't get to. I was not excluded by them as they expressed their joy, but they were happier than I was. You could see and hear and feel their happiness, but I just wasn't there like they were. What was I missing? What was I lacking? I believe today, looking backward, that I had lost the childhood that they were enjoying. I had been forced to grow up in an instant at age ten, and, after that, there was no going back to childhood innocence.

In creative writing, I tried to express myself, and I thought about writing a fictional piece about sex abuse by a priest. In the mid-1960s, it would probably have blown up in my face. I felt that I wouldn't be able to get away with pretending the abuse had happened to "John Doe." I thought that my teacher would send me to the office after reading my story. I was, and still am, the world's worst liar. Even the littlest white lie shows on my face. I did, however, write a short story for myself, which I tore up upon completion, afraid that someone would find it and read it.

I liked acting in plays more than anything else. I had trained myself into becoming an Oscar-worthy actor. With ease, I could pretend to be anybody else. The directors of our plays took note of that ability, and they told some of my fellow actors to watch how I was able to get into character with such ease. Those many hours in the back of my closet or at my desk with the dim light were my stage. At those times, I would become someone else—anyone but Charles.

Charles was, after all, a bad person—very bad. I became my own talk show host, a radio personality, a soldier behind enemy lines, and scores of other characters. The back of the closet became my own world that Neary could not reach. One of my favorite make-believe roles was to be a pilot. I flew around the world, visiting faraway countries. I went to remote places—places that no one else had ever been to. I even flew back in time to the days of the old wild-Western cowboys, or into the future to my own private, distant planet.

I remained on the fringe, the edge, where I grew up faster than my numbered years. What was your childhood like? Were you with me on the edge, or were you one of those fortunate ones who felt unbridled excitement after your school team won a football game? What was that excitement like?

What is the key to being "in," to truly feeling that you are a part of things? Even today, I still view many things from the edge.

24

HEALING SERVICES

In a move to extend healing, the bishop has held healing services. I didn't name them "healing" services—the bishop named them. There was a healing service in Oswego, New York, that I heard of after it had occurred. The paper noted that there would be one held at Holy Family Church, in Fairmount soon. It is a neighboring town, not far from us. Sue and I decided to go.

It was in January, and we were having one of our blizzards with very heavy snow. We got there early, and we saw only a few cars. There was about forty-five minutes before it was to start, so Sue and I decided to go to a nearby store and window-shop. Maybe there would be more cars there when we returned.

We arrived back at the church, and only a few cars were there, as the snow fell at a rapid rate. I took a deep breath, and Sue helped me in the side door. We looked around the church and saw only a handful of people. Had the snow kept them away? Had their fear kept them away? What was it? Where were they?

As we sat waiting for the service to start, I became nervous. We sat in the second row, almost center. I looked around me, and memories of my abuse haunted me once again. While this church building was not here when my abuse started and I was not here with Neary, it still triggered memories. I reflected on other victims I had met and how they were raped right on the altars of their own churches. Some of them were altar boys, and they were abused before or after mass.

An altar boy walked right in front of us as we sat there. I began to shake, sweat, and become very uneasy. I felt frozen in my seat. Sue had never seen me like this, and she held me. She could feel me shake, and she sensed my fear. She asked if I wanted to go or stay. In my mind, I wanted to bolt out of there as if I was on fire, but I also felt a need to stay. If I left, the abusers would have won another round, and I would have lost again.

The bishop and several priests came down the aisle. We scanned the crowd. Well, "crowd" is not the word—there were maybe fifteen people in this church that could seat hundreds. Where were all the people?

Sue asked me again if I wanted to leave, as I shook uncontrollably. I could not move. My legs would not work, and I couldn't get up, even with her help. I continued to shake, sweat, and wring my hands.

The bishop looked out over the few, very few, and said how he felt bad about the actions of his fellow clergy. He prayed for them and their victims. Then there was a long period of silent reflection. Then the bishop said some closing prayers. I don't know what I expected, but this wasn't it.

I had met with the bishop many times, and I had said that the gap between me and God was hurtful and needed repair. The loss of God is so painful. There had to be something that could narrow this chasm created years before by one of his priests.

Sue told me that we could leave, right then, if I wanted, but I was frozen, still frozen and shaking. I couldn't get up. *It will be over soon* (that is the same thing I thought when Neary was raping me), *just hang in there, and it will soon end.*

As the priests and the bishop left the altar and walked down the aisle next to us, the bishop didn't even glance my way. He surely knew that I was there because our eyes had made contact more than once during the "healing," yet he walked right by me.

Sue saw red. He would not get away with this. I was visibly shaking and hurt. She left my side and followed them into the room they changed in. She took the bishop by the arm and said that he needed to come out and see me, right now. And he said, "You mean Charles?" Sue said yes. While this was going on, the victims advocate for the diocese came and sat with me. She tried to calm me down, and then Sue appeared with the bishop. He came and sat with me. I told him how I felt alone and separate from God and how I felt too dirty for God's love. The news media was there, and they took a photo of me and him, which was published in the next day's paper.

We spoke of God and of my hurt. I also asked him how could he keep the list of the forty-nine accused priests to himself. After all, the Bishops' Charter for the Protection of Children and Young People clearly dictates complete openness and transparency. This, I felt he was not living up to. He stated that, by canon law, he could not speak ill of another priest, and also, because of the Catholic Church's eighth commandment not to bear false witness against your neighbor, he felt that he could not reveal the names. I told him that I didn't believe that's what Jesus would do. He stood his ground, and to this day, he won't speak of the names on the list of forty-nine.

Both he and the victim assistance coordinator wanted to know what they could do to draw out more victims. They felt that the healing service would bring more out. I told them that the idea was good, but the location was poor. To draw out the broken and hurting victims, the setting of the service would have to be at a neutral place, not in the church proper. Many victims will never enter a church again because many of them were abused in the church. That is the last place where they would show up.

The bishop and the victim assistance coordinator pledged to work with me to see how and where we could have a healing service and draw victims out. As I said in my chapter on triggers, the vestments also spook many victims, myself included, because their abusers wore their full black garb during the abusive acts. Many feel the same as I do about a loss of God and its associated emptiness. Where was God? Where is God now? The answers will never be found in the church proper.

Another attempt at healing took place at a retreat outside Rochester, New York. It was attended by less than one hundred people. Once again, I was left empty. When I asked the bishop about prayer, his response was very hurtful. I asked him, "Why did God not answer my prayer when I was but ten years old and hurt? I asked God to end my pain, to take Neary by stroke, heart attack, or accident, or if he couldn't take him, please take me. Was I truly worthless, no need to answer my prayers? Did I not say the right words? Did I say them in the wrong order? Why had God not answered my prayers?" The bishop looked at me with his cold, dark eyes and said, "People pray for peace every day and you don't see that either, do you?" I said to myself, *Boy, do I feel better now. Thanks for nothing, Bishop! I'm so glad to see your compassion for victims of sexual abuse by clergy.*

25

GUILT

Guilt—this is a tough one. If you have not "been there, suffered from that," then you might have a hard time seeing things from my side. As an adult, looking backward in time to when my abuse started, I felt guilt. At least, that is the word most of us use to describe what we feel. It has taken the better part of three years of self-evaluation, aided by my wife and Dr. Driscoll, to get where I am now.

Guilt. Let's take a moment and look at it. Guilt. The way it rolls off your tongue—guilt—it conveys something bad just by saying it. It takes a long time, a very long time, to let go of the feeling of guilt. As we age, we know that the things we were forced to do by these evildoers have caused us to feel guilt.

All that any one of us victims is actually guilty of is being a child. We have no guilt; we were kids! Guilt as an adult is a good thing. Guilt shows its face when we are about to do something that, at some level we know is wrong, and the guilt feelings are our final warning signal to do what is right and not let history repeat itself.

What many of us victims have felt over the years is really regret. Dr. Driscoll has convinced me of that. We, as adults, regret actions that happened *to us*—not *by us*. While this concept looks good on paper and sounds good to hear, it is still a hard thing to buy into.

It was far from an even match. Adult clergy against an innocent child. No match there at all. That is why it felt like my perpetrator had more than two hands. That is why it felt like I was being strangled by a huge, constricting snake. The more I struggled, the tighter his grip became, and it was difficult at times to even breathe. As my little lungs exhaled, his grip felt ever tighter, making each breath harder than the one before.

Regret in my situation means that I wish something had never happened, but I was powerless to stop it. I confess to being guilty of playing the what-if or only-if game in my head a million times. *If only I had done this or done that, and what if I* … stop it. Tell yourself to stop it. I have to keep telling myself to stop it, as the adult looks backward to the unknowing child. The more adult survivors I meet, the more I see a common thread among us. We all look back and Monday-morning quarterback ourselves.

This brings me to "forgiveness." Those of us abused by clergy are being told at every turn that we must forgive our predators. That they need to be forgiven. I will never forgive Neary. To me, forgiveness requires that the abuser admit to the crime committed (in this case, a felony crime), and that he ask for my forgiveness. While my wife and doctor would attest to me not forgiving him, it is not something that I harbor and allow to fester in a deep crevasse. I also don't wear my refusal to forgive as a badge on my sleeve for all to see. I do, however, convert my feelings to controlled anger, in little slices, as to not overload. This anger motivates me to tell this account of my abuse and to extend myself to those left in the wake of their abuse, thinking that there is no one out there who cares.

I will say that I have forgiven myself now, after much therapy, because I truly was helpless when the abuse occurred. The problem is that those of us who look back at what happened are looking through our adult eyes and not through our childhood eyes. Once that is realized, we can begin to forgive ourselves. Forgive Neary? Not a chance. Does God forgive him? Only he knows that, and he and I are on shaky ground still, although I'm working on that. Whether I forgive Neary or not doesn't really mean anything. It is in God's hands now, and I trust that he will sit in judgment of Neary. Neary will have to account for his deeds here on Earth to God. He escaped both criminal and civil punishment, as so many others do, due to statute of limitations time constraints. Isn't it a little ironic that there is supposed to be a separation of church and state, until the church needs something like the statute of limitations to hide behind?

I'm not saying that others should not forgive their perpetrators. I'm only saying that I won't forgive mine. I see no need to. Do I forgive God? That is the bigger question. Being raised Catholic, it should strike fear in me to question God, but it doesn't. I believe that he wants us to question him and his power or presence. Didn't he walk the Earth trying to convince people of his importance? He didn't punish those who wondered and asked questions. I still seek God to this very minute. I have spoken to dozens of clergy, telling them, above all, that I want God back in my life, and it is a constant struggle to find that path. They have sent me down many paths, but they dead-end, and I am left with more questions than answers. However, there is one exception; my daughter's minister in North Carolina has helped me in my search, although the physical distance between us breaks up the process. We've called and written each other, but face-to-face contact is best for an exchange of this nature.

I don't want to leave this life not having a firm base and a reconnection to God, as my connection was severed, not by me, but by another. I still feel that an indelible stain was put on my soul as a youngster, which remains there today. *God, can you hear me? Hello? Hello? This is Charles, still asking questions. Do you love me at all? Even a little maybe?*

26

GOD, CHURCH, PRAYER, AND THE EVIL PRIESTS

That title sounds like a mouthful, doesn't it? The first three things get damaged, sometimes forever, by the last one. The first three make for a good life. The fourth makes you question the first three.

God, we are taught, created us in his image and his likeness, and he dwells within us. I feel that that is an ideal, and I would love it to be that way. Survivors of abuse, I believe, struggle more with this side of life.

We are told that when two or more of us gather in God's name, then they are in church. Think about that. The God, the Jesus, whom I used to pray to, stood on a grassy knoll overlooking the masses and preached the word. He was not in an ornate building with all the excess; it was just him and the multitudes.

Prayer is the link, the direct link, to express ourselves to God. We pray to him and ask him for forgiveness for the wrongs that we have committed. We ask for help in times of trial and sickness. We turn to him for support and encouragement. Does prayer really work? I can't answer that one easily. A priest who was part of a group I spoke before recently asked if he could send me a book to read. He said it was called *Angry with God*.

I read the book. I didn't get much relief from it. I find that I can't express myself to God without yelling at him or to him. Being "born Catholic," as my mother tells me I was, I feel very conflicted. The book did say that it is OK to be angry with God; it is even OK to yell at him. It's not like he can't take it. So, I let go of a little guilt about my feelings toward God.

Because I had a short, first marriage as a teenager that was blessed by the Catholic Church, I could not be married in the Catholic Church the second time around. While Sue desired to be married in the Catholic Church, it was not a deal breaker to be married in the Methodist Church. My mother called frequently to ask if we would seek an annulment and be remarried in the Catholic

Church. She would never let it go. Sue and I joined a United Methodist church. We were happy there, but Mom stayed on my case about it. I gave in to the pressure, and Sue and I looked into an annulment. We made an appointment with the local Catholic priest. Seeing that collar up close again terrified me. Sue knew that I was uncomfortable, but not why. I talked fast and was told that we needed cash to get it started. This offended both Sue and I. I looked at the picture of the Pope on the wall, surrounded by gold and jewels and thought why do they need my money to fix a mistake that I made? We were also told to get five people to come forward and answer to the church's tribunal board, as to where the blame lay for the failure of my first marriage. I asked the priest about Jesus. I asked about Jesus leaving the flock for a single sheep to be brought back, but this priest would only let me back if I paid him. How could this be? If I had the cash, I could be Catholic again? In addition to two collections during Mass, when I was young, my mother-in-law said she also had a coupon book with payments due to the church, which were expected to be paid also.

Money is the root of all evil? The Catholic Church is the root of what? You decide. For the right amount of cash, Sue and I could be married in the Catholic Church, and then we could stop living in sin. Tell me it's not all about cash with the Catholic Church.

The shepherd left his flock of sheep to find the one that strayed, we were told. We try to come back from being lost and are told to bring our checkbook. When Sue and I got home, my mother offered to pay the money that was needed to become Catholic again. And, of course, the answer was no. We raised our four children Methodist. The kids went to Sunday school, and they later went to the church. Three were baptized in this church. We attended church there for almost twenty years. Pastors came and went, some to retirement and others to other churches. We remained.

I truly expected my church to come to me in my time of need. My pastor did come to my house after my most recent neck surgery. When asked how I was doing other than my surgery, I spoke of my childhood sexual abuse by a Catholic priest. He admitted knowledge of my abuse. He had seen the newspaper articles from months ago. Sadly, that was that. He left saying that he would come back, but he never did. In the spring, at the time of the article, he stopped me on the way out of church and said that he would call me and set a lunch date. That, too, never happened.

There are good clergy out there, but they are very few, out of the dozens who have crossed my path. Steve Matthews in North Carolina is one of the good ones. He is a very passionate man, deeply devoted to the word of God. I gave him my business card one day after church. We were visiting our children and grandchildren at the time, and we attended our daughter Tracy's church. I asked Tracy if it was all right to give him my card and ask him one question. I didn't want to jeopardize her connection to his church.

I felt like we were welcomed into her church, and that they would be there in our times of need. In September of 2003, I had yet another cervical spine surgery. This time, titanium rods and screws were used to try and stabilize my vertebrae. The doctor who performed the delicate surgery was Dr. Winfield. He said, "I am going to speak the truth to you. Some things you will like, and others you will not. If I only speak the truth, I never have to remember what I said when next we meet." Boy, is that a mouthful. That is quite a gem to live by, I feel. It is so simple, yet so true. I try to do the same. The truth can be extremely painful and hard, or it can be reassuring and good. Speak the truth, and you never have to remember what you said. If it needs to be restated, just tell the truth again. Dr. Winfield is an extremely talented surgeon. He has taken many tough cases—some other doctors wouldn't touch. He thanks God for the talent he has, and I thank him and God. I would not be walking, or worse, if it weren't for Dr. Winfield.

So many people come up to Sue and me saying that they attend the best church with the best clergymen. To make a long story short, we sold some winter gear to a person who had heard about me from the TV and newspaper and had recommended his pastor. I continue my search to close the void between me and God, so I took his name and phone number. A few days passed, and we connected to arrange to meet the next day for lunch so I could share with him my concerns about God. He asked for some specifics, as he wanted to prepare something to speak with me about. I gave him the five-minute, PG-rated version of why I wanted to meet. We were to have lunch the next day, but something came up, and he cancelled on me. OK, things happen. I called him again for another date, and he never got back to me. Is God truly the only one who goes after the lost sheep? These situations do two things to me. First, they galvanize my feeling that I am too dirty for God's love, and, second, they cause me to believe once more that there aren't many clergy who really care.

I have been heading in the direction of a more personal relationship with God. I have eliminated the middleman, if you will. It is between me and him. I still talk to him, most of the time not in an organized prayer mode, but more by open conversing in nature. The "Lord's Prayer" or "Our Father" cannot be said in my presence. As I have said before, I was abused to that prayer, with my abuser repeating the "thy will be done" verse while I was being raped, and the prayer still pulls me to a painful place I'd rather not be in.

Prayer, to pray. Why? What for? Why pray? I don't know. If we love God, then he knows it. If we hate God, then he knows it. If we are indifferent, then God knows this too. Don't you remember being taught that God is, was, and always will be? That God is all-powerful and all-knowing? Being raised Catholic; we were taught that over and over. But is it true? We won't know until we leave this world.

Prayer—didn't Jesus say on the cross something like, "Father, why do you forsake me?" God let him suffer, his only son, a terrible, painful death. If God would not interfere to aid his own son, why would he help you and me through prayer? He didn't' even help his own son. Being "all-powerful," God could save us from our sins in other ways than allowing Jesus to be nailed to a cross to die.

It makes my blood boil when people say they prayed for a material thing and, if it came to be, they thank God for answering their prayers. Look around you, read the papers, watch the news, educate yourself, and then think, *did God really help me to get that new microwave or that financing for a new car?*

Church, the Catholic Church, has many facets. I remember being away at college, and the church was almost three miles from the dorms. I walked one Sunday morning to attend the church with one of my classmates. When we got there and walked in the door, there was a man standing there in his suit. There was also a small box that said on it "Pew Fee, 50 Cents." We walked by because we had no money. We sat down. Moments passed, and then this man tapped me on the shoulder and said I hadn't paid the pew fee. I told him that I had no money. He told me and my classmate that we would have to leave if we didn't pay. We left. It's awful that the Catholic Church would charge admission to come and worship God.

Some of the warped logic that we get from the Church makes one scratch one's head. "The meanings of celibacy—a priest who was arrested in 2002 on a sex charge claimed that he was celibate since he had never married and only had sexual relations with 'four women and ten men' since his ordination. He asserted that these acts were simply 'sins' against chastity and did not violate his celibate vow. This patent rationalization is not uncommon. It reflects the attitude that bishops have registered in cases of offending priests" (Sipe 25–26).

I left the Catholic Church? I wouldn't necessarily put it that way. I feel that I just stopped going. The sight of the Roman collar did not trigger me back then as it does now because it was much later that I realized that Neary was not an anomaly, but rather one of thousands of bad priests. In the late summer of 1969, I left home to attend college many miles away—about a four-hour drive. When Sunday came, I spent it studying and doing homework assignments. My mom wasn't there to prod me on to get up and go to church.

27

THE VOYAGE FROM VICTIM TO SURVIVOR

The voyage from victim to survivor. It is truly a voyage in every sense of the word. The sad part, the very sad part, is that many of us don't make it. Success on your voyage is easier with help. Professional help is best, if you can obtain it. Approach your bishop and victims assistance coordinator. Support from loved ones is not always there. I am lucky. I have a very good doctor and very supportive wife and children. If you have neither, don't despair. There are victim support groups nationwide. Approach SNAP at www.snapnetwork.org and search for a group in your area. If there is none local to you, contact the closest group leader. There may be one coming your way, or the local leader may help you on a peer counseling level. The SNAP leader may also know of a professional who may be able to help you and agree on a fee that you can afford.

It is so sad for those of us who don't make it. Too many cut their lives short under the pressure. They take their own lives. Don't get ahead of me, however, as it is not just the abused child who ends his or her life; adults who were victims also break down. Some don't make it to "survivorhood."

I would have been one of those unknown statistics—one whom people would have wondered about. I would have never left a note to explain what was done to me—only that God didn't love me. Remember, it was done to us, *not* by us, because we were only kids when it happened. I carefully plotted ways to kill Neary and myself many, many times. However, being a child, I could not carry them out. I would still daydream, however, of which tree we could hit along the road, as we drove to a house where he would abuse me. I would guess when just the right moment would be to pull hard on the steering wheel to try to hit the tree and kill us both. One thing that stopped me from trying this was the worry of only hurting myself and not being killed. I wanted to be dead. I wanted him to be dead.

The hundreds of notes I did write were never read by anyone. I would toss them out shortly after writing them. I viewed myself as a coward and a chicken. After all, why couldn't I follow through?

In the past three-plus years, I have met many victims and some victim/survivors and some survivors. These are stages we go through. We start out being victims. We then start on our personal journeys and are part victim, part survivor. If our goal is achieved, we are survivors. I look back at my journey to date; I feel the victim I see over my shoulder is getting ever smaller, and the survivor still in front of me is getting closer. I do believe that the voyage from victim to survivor must take place in each of us, by each of us, with support during our rocky times. I believe that there are really three stages we voyage through in our search for peace.

I know some people, as do you, who will live and die at the victim stage. It is truly sad and disheartening. Their fragile lives are broken, broken beyond repair, like a dropped glass on a stone floor. They are in emotional pieces, scattered about, and in some cases, they have no one to help gather them up. Since the day they became victims, their lives were shattered forever. I can't stress enough to get professional help. If the first, second, or third attempt to find the right doctor fails, still keep trying; they are out there.

Speaking for myself, I became a victim that fall day of 1961. I stayed a victim until the spring of 2002, Memorial Day weekend, when I could hold it in no longer. That day began a long journey from victim to where I am right now. I am in the victim/survivor stage—if I were to rate myself. My goal is to be a survivor.

I work hard with my doctor and with my number one ally, my wife, Sue. The pace of the voyage will vary. Not only from person to person, but also in the same person. It depends on how you process what you're going through. I have good days and bad. I have good hours and bad in the same day. There is no cookbook recipe to follow, no framework, that works for everyone.

There are so many degrees of sexual abuse and of sexual abuse at the hands of clergy. While no abuse should ever be tolerated, it steps it up a notch when the abuser is a family friend and a priest. Where can you turn? Not to your faith, because it is your faith that got you there.

The Boston lawyers had to find a way to prorate the settlement among the victims. They had to address degrees of abuse to determine an equitable division of the monies. Think of it this way: given that there should be no sexual abuse as a starting point, follow along here. Suppose those of us who have been sexually abused by clergy were riding in a car. The car swerves off the road and hits a tree. All of us were in an accident, just like all of us were sexually abused. However, all our injuries are different. Some might have come through the car wreck with only scrapes, others might have needed medical attention for broken bones, and still others might have lived a few days but then they died from their injuries. Some might have instantly died in the crash itself. We were all "abused" in the wreck, but to differing degrees. The same is true of our experiences with abusive clergy. It is a fact that our experiences are alike and different at the same time. We all rode in that car, but we each came out of it with different injuries.

I read and hear many testimonies of others' sexual abuse by clergy, and the common thread with us all (in addition to the act) is the need for God, in some manner and to some degree, to aid us.

This need is always with us, but, no, I don't believe we dwell on it. However, as I said in the chapter on triggers, we do not know what will bring it back. The quiet, peaceful times can be suddenly overrun with memories, which we wish would never come back. I have to admit to times when I feel that a flood of tears is only a blink of an eye away. It lingers just out of sight. I can feel the tears swell up in me, as I know they do in other victims too. You can't predict it, you can't stop it, and you have to hold on and ride it out. Sometimes the tears do start streaming down my cheeks when I find no conscious reason for them, when the physical part of my being is telling me that the emotional part needs a little hug, a little reassurance, or even a soft touch on the shoulder from a loved one. Sue is very tuned into me, and she mostly knows when I am starting down that path. I weep, not just for me, but for all of us victims and for those who are being abused by clergy right now as you hold this book. It is awful.

Recently, I met a victim who was just holding on by his fingernails. He had been abused by a priest at an early age, and he had told this priest's superior, only to be raped by the superior. Then he had told the bishop, only to be raped by the bishop. The truth is stranger than any fiction we could think up. I sat across the table from him, and there was a look, a damaged look, in his eyes. He was a very broken man—maybe beyond repair. As Sue and I sat with him, we tried to extend help, but like so many others, it was not to be. He drifted off to parts unknown, and we can't find him.

The sickening thing about this is that there are no "do overs" in real life. Once you've been raped by a priest, you view the entire world differently from those who escaped sexual abuse. You regard problems and arrive at decisions from places that others don't. An example is a forwarded e-mail that I got about the World Trade Center tragedy recently. It spoke of things like losing your keys, getting tied up in traffic, missing your bus, getting a flat tire, oversleeping your alarm, or a child's illness causing you to stay home. Then it went on to say that you should not be upset when these things happen to you, as they happened to some of those who were saved from death at the World Trade Center. The e-mail said that "God" had put these people where he wanted them to be, and so they were spared. The moral is to not be upset by life's little stumbling blocks. The next time you lose your keys, etc., don't be upset, God has a plan. OK, do you feel good, a little bit? At first, maybe yes, but then what about the thousands who perished that day? Were they also where God wanted them to be? Were their deaths part of "the plan" that day too? Not if we're talking about the God I struggle to pray to.

Different points of view—we all have them, but some are more extreme than others. A few days ago, there was a young boy of twelve who hanged himself. He had attended a Catholic school. What could bring a young boy to feel that life is that worthless? We will never know, but many of us can surmise a scenario, can't we? I had never heard of this boy before, and don't know the particulars, but I wept for him.

This is so tragic. Life is so fragile; it can so easily slip away from us. Signs? Sure there are signs before someone takes their life. The hard part is to see them. The signs may be very subtle. The signs may not be visible to the naked eye. We carry our feelings deep inside—so deep that we are afraid to let them out.

I have said that I am afraid of my anger. I am afraid of my rage. I need to let it out in controlled doses; I feel that if I let it out unchecked, the results would be awful. Channeling the anger and rage is the answer. You need a professional to help you learn how to do this. Slowly, ever so slowly, my anger, my rage, is being used for "good" and not for "evil." Sue and Dr. Driscoll will tell you how passionate I am to do all I can to stop the sexual abuse of all children. It is my mission in life. I not only want to aid others on their journeys from victim to survivor, but I also want to try to prevent further abuses.

It is said that sexual abuse of children is not about the sex, but rather about the power. Let me set the record straight on that one. While I will accept that power is a component, it is just that; it's only a component. There came a time between the fall of 1961 and spring of 1963 when I stopped trying to fight Father Neary off. I was so little and he was so big. My struggling only hurt me more physically. The more I fought, the more that it hurt me, not him. I got to the point where I offered very little resistance. It hurt less that way; after all, it was not like he wasn't going to get what he came for. I went inward. I turned into myself and moved mentally elsewhere. While he could ravage my body and my very soul, I made a safe place to retreat to in my head for me, just for me. No one was allowed to go there but me. That was the only control that I really had.

The abuse was about the sex. As much as it was about the power he got from it. After I gave in to ease my physical pain, he would be having the time of his life back there, moaning, groaning, smiling, and dripping sweat onto me. He was truly enjoying himself, as I could see his reflection in my wall mirror. He could have cared less that I was emotionless and that I was not fighting him anymore. I had developed a "give in, get it over" attitude. There were times that he barely spoke ten words to me. He would just get his pleasure and then be gone. That is why I say that he was evil and not sick. I have looked evil directly in the face—a level of evil worse than any horror movie could show you.

An aspect of the abuses that gets very little coverage is the tremendous pleasure of "the hunt," as I call it. Neary got just as much pleasure from the hunt of his prey (me) as he did from the rape itself. I can clearly see, looking back, how he had laid the groundwork before he pounced. I can remember the disturbing look coming from his eyes that told me that there was more than a car ride coming, but I didn't know what. You know the feeling when the hairs stand up on the back of your neck, but you aren't sure why? I now know why. I can swear there was saliva dripping from the corners of his mouth as he surveyed me, his prey. He was waiting, grooming, planning, and moving in slowly, until *bam*, he jumped me. I was his prize, his reward, his toy. These priests do not perform random acts on us. If anything, child sex abuse by priests is probably the most carefully planned out attack of any crime.

Yes, back to crimes. To this day, no, to this minute, if you pick up a paper, watch the TV news, or read a magazine, there will be something about one of us victims being belittled by the Church calling the abuse a sin. It is so very sad, because that so-called "sin" is not only a crime, but also a felony. The abuse is viewed by our Catholic leaders as a sin, and then they claim that they can't commit another sin by talking about it. Does anyone think that this is what Jesus would do?

This voyage I travel will most likely have no conclusion. I say that because I want what I can never have. I want what money can't buy. I want my childhood back, unblemished by the vile acts of a priest. I want to grow up, not on the fringe, but as a genuine part of my peer group. So many feel that we want money. Who is more deserving of a settlement than a young boy, or young girl, who was raped of his or her innocence as a child? It is not like a sprained ankle that happened years ago. The abuse is a permanent scar to my being, right down to and including my soul. I still feel that Neary put a permanent stain on my soul that exists today. It is indelible; it cannot be erased or covered up. I continue to search for God and for his forgiveness of the stain. I tread lightly in my search, ever so lightly, as I am afraid of what I might find. Suppose that what I fear is true? Suppose there really is a stain on my soul placed there by a "man of God"? Maybe I'm not worthy of God's love. Maybe, just maybe, he's not there …

Weekly, if not daily I get phone calls, cards, letters, or e-mails from fellow victims. Sometimes I get a thirty-second call, but other times it's a call that lasts for several hours. Some tell me their names, and others wish to remain anonymous. I tell them that is OK, that it is not about what you want to be known by. Some calls are words of thanks for doing a TV interview, or a newspaper article, or a speaking engagement. They, too, have suffered the same fate, but cannot step forward and be counted. They, too, carry the pain and guilt they don't deserve. Some are onetime contacts, and others maintain contact, but from a distance. Others join my local SNAP chapter.

A man called me the other day and told me how he is tortured by memories of his abuse. They came flooding back, he said, due to recent coverage in the media. He wanted to keep the memories put away, as did I. I told him that I've been where he was. I told him that it feels like treading on thin ice with golf cleats on, you're just waiting for the ice to crack and then you will fall through and disappear forever. It is truly scary, but there is help. Will he come forward? Will he seek help? I hope so. I, too, suffered in silence way too long. There is a part of you that looks back and tries to believe that it never happened. Take it from me—that doesn't work.

I have long felt like I am only on the shoreline of life. My voyage has yet to unfold before me. As I sit on the shore, I look out into the lake of life and see people, many people. They are enjoying themselves and each other. They interact and laugh, truly laugh, and it's not like the forced laughter that I do to save face at gatherings. They play in the lake of life. Sure, the water gets rough from time to time, as I sit there on the shore, watching them, longing to belong. When rough water hits, they band together until the lake is calm once again. I reach out mentally, trying to see just how and what they do. I squint, I strain, but I can't quite see. I can hear their interaction, and I look to my left and my right. As I look down the shoreline of this lake of life, I see many like me. Some are sitting, and their toes may be getting wet, and others sit farther back so as to avoid any contact with the water. I can see their faces clearly. They are like me. They are my people. They are fellow sexual abuse victims. I see the longing in their eyes and faces. They, too, want to join the others. One gets the courage, and we all watch with anticipation to see his progress. Can he make it in the lake of life? Can he be with the others? As I gaze up and down this shoreline, I see all eyes glued on the one of us who has dared enter the lake. He enters the water, but it only gets deeper, and he disappears below the surface, never to be seen again. We look to each other on the shoreline, next to the lake of life, and then away, lest we make eye contact, and see each other's hurt. Maybe, next time, maybe then I will be the one to get the courage to try to join the others in the lake of life, or maybe I too will perish before I reach them, as countless others have done before me.

My journey, from victim to survivor. It is long and difficult. Each inch is hard. I can only move forward by looking back.

28

HOW SUPPORT HELPS

I have always viewed my mom from a different angle than my four siblings viewed her. My perception was that they were more connected to Mom than I was, without any effort on their part. I am not the middle child with middle-child syndrome. I am the fourth of five. My mom's health has deteriorated, being eighty-seven this year, and she cannot live alone any longer. My younger brother, who lives in Nevada, took her in because his house is on one floor with no steps. We just found out that she has a brain tumor about the size of a thumb. There is a long list of other problems regarding her health, and her days are numbered. I told Kevin that when he felt her time was short, to let me know.

A few weeks ago, she was hospitalized. Her kidneys weren't working, and a myriad of other things were piling up. Kevin said that this would be the time he would pick to come see her. So after much "do I go, or do I wait" wondering, I decided to go. Kevin, after all, is an RN, and he is planning to become a physician's assistant. His medical knowledge comes from years of practice.

I told Dr. Driscoll and Sue that I wanted something from her, but I didn't' know what. What could I ask her and what if I hated the answer? This past Christmas, I had sent her a note telling her that what I wished for her for Christmas was for her to let go of her guilt about what happened to me, even though it had occurred right under her nose. I have to believe that she would have intervened, had she known. She's my mom after all. Mothers protect their children at any cost, in my head anyway. I see how Sue has been an outstanding mom to our four children. She would have bare-handed intervened with anyone who would have caused her children harm, and today, she still would intervene for our grandchildren. That's the kind of mom I wanted. We can't pick our moms, though, and I do have to say that mine loved me deeply. Being the only sibling who stayed in Syracuse, New York, as the other four moved away, I had more contact with mom and dad than they did. I did have more "face time" than my siblings did. I was always there for mom and dad, and Sue would attest to that.

I flew out to Nevada to see her. She was very happy to see me. She hugged me and cried, as I hugged her in her hospital bed. If her blood count rose, she would be able to come home to Kevin's house and have an aide stay with her while Kevin worked. That was the goal. A few days later, she came home, and I sat with her. What was it I wanted to ask? Did I want to tell her something instead of asking her a question? She still says how awful my experiences as a child were, and how she wished she could take my pain away—both my physical and my emotional pain. She has said many times how sorry she is to have not seen the signs. She is sorry that she blindly believed Rev. Neary's reasons why I would be upset. I know her apologies are sincere because when she first found out, she would call me, crying and saying that she was so sorry. You can't fake that kind of apology.

Why was I there? I asked her no questions; she said nothing profound to me. It was peaceful. I sat next to her at times and just held her trembling hand, telling her it was OK. They say people know when their time is short, and I think she knows. Her bedtime is difficult. She cries because she's afraid of passing in her sleep.

I listened to her talk of the old days when she was young, and she drifted. Sometimes she did not know where she was or who we were. For moments in time, she was very lucid, and then, minutes later, she would forget almost everything. Her brain tumor was taking its toll. She was too frail for surgery and has heart problems and a long list of other problems. She is not a candidate for surgery.

As the week passed and I sat with her, sometimes in silence, I felt a renewed sense of our mother-son bond. It probably sounds a little wacky, but as I held her hand and tried to comfort her, I felt a sense of peace. There was nothing that I wanted to ask her. There was nothing that I wanted to say other than "I love you too, Mom." I thought that it was the last time that I would see her alive, and she wept the morning I left for home. Still trembling and ever so frail, she hugged me hard and said good-bye. I kissed her on the cheek and told her that I loved her.

I came home with a sense of finality toward Mom. We had made peace with each other without any words being exchanged, and it was OK. The OK feeling is new to me. I feel that it is truer each time that I think it now. I am OK.

My life with Sue is solid. She not only understands me, but she is like a pit bull to anyone she feels might try to harm me. On one speaking engagement before a group of Catholics at a Voice of the Faithful meeting, a plain-clothed priest sat in back. I saw how he was kind of smirking, with a "yeah, right" attitude showing. Sue picked up on it and gave him a tongue-lashing. Here I am trying to educate these interested Catholics in what and how the abuse happens, and he is smiling. She told him, "Mister, take that smirk off your face!" Sue is one amazing woman. If I could pick anyone, anywhere, I would still pick Sue.

I am very happy for the unconditional love I receive from my children and now from my eight grandchildren. It humbles me. I sometimes wonder what they see in me. I have felt like damaged goods for so many years, that a part of me feels that I don't deserve this unconditional love, even from my daughters-in-law and son-in-law. I had a great fear that I would be rejected by them, even if my kids still accepted me, now that they all knew my story. I wish I could change the hurt I have seen in their eyes and the tears they have shed upon learning what had happened to me. I now know that it was a sign of their deep, unconditional love—something I have not felt worthy of. Even two of my three brothers-in-law and their spouses showed me this kind of love. My brother-in-law Dave even carries my business card and speaks the truth of this evil to those who mock it or make little of it. Dave says that he knows about this type of abuse, as he knows my life. Again, I feel a little humbled that here is my brother-in-law, trying to fight the fight and defend me from thousands of miles away. Why does Dave do this for me? Dave does it because he loves me and is there for me when needed.

I truly am lovable, and it's taking me awhile to accept the fact. I still look out from inside, where my scars are, and I wonder how could this love be? The mental beating I had from the early age of ten left a deep chasm in my mind, convincing me that I was not worthy of love and that God didn't love me, and making me question why anyone else should love me. After thinking that time after time, it becomes who you are—a person whom no one would want. That is quite a wall to climb over or knock down. It is a daunting task. That's why I strongly urge to all victims to get professional help. If you take nothing else from me in this book, take away the part about getting professional help. I admit, too, that I was skeptical about getting professional help at first.

I really thought that the doctor would sit in judgment of me, as the Church has sometimes done. All too often, the Church tells one of us that we need to go to confession for what we have "done," or we need to pray for our perpetrators, as they need more help than we do. The Catholic Church still doesn't get it. Where are the Catholics? Where is their outrage? The Voice of the Faithful group say to keep the faith, but change the Church. That is pretty much it. It comes down to accountability and justice. These priests didn't relocate themselves; their bishops moved them. It is well documented that the bishops played the "move the priest game." As we all know, that just gives the priests a new group of children to "prey upon" instead of doing what they should be doing, which is to "pray upon" the children. There is a saying "No Justice, No Healing, Know Justice, Know Healing." I saw this on a bumper sticker.

It is sickening to compare the handful of priests who have been made accountable for their deeds to those still out there. It doesn't seem to me that Jesus would hide behind the "statute of limitations," as the Church has done. At least not the Jesus I pray to. It is past the time to make the bishops accountable for their actions, time limit or not. Why aren't Catholics outraged by this? Don't they want their church to be rid of this evil? Just because time has passed, it does not mean that nothing happened and that no accountability is needed. It only means that the priests escaped possible prosecution. Our children are our most precious little people, and they need protection from this evil—nothing less. Performing a volunteer self-study, which is what the 2004 audit by the church really was, does little. These priests would all pass the background checks, as they were never turned over to the authorities. They have no record. The so-called "audit" is a shameful whitewash at best. The "audit" could be trusted if it was truly independent and not by someone selected and paid for by the church. Remember Enron? Remember when they were caught with their financial accounting errors? Were they allowed to hire their own group to "audit" themselves? Was Enron allowed to self-investigate the "problem"? Were they allowed to decide what, if anything needed fixing? No. A resounding no. Why, then, was the Catholic Church allowed the luxury to investigate the possibility of felony crimes being committed and whether enough time had passed so that they could hide behind the statute of limitations? This sexual abuse by priests on small children is a felony crime, plain and simple. Now back on topic.

I would be remiss if I didn't mention my other mom, my mother-in-law, Barbara. While a little skeptical at first, she is now angry and disillusioned about my story. She was converted to Catholicism when she married her husband. She raised her kids Catholic. She has also wept for me and has come to see me speak. I can see where Sue got her compassion from. Barbara is truly more than a mother-in-law. She would do anything she could to help rid this evil.

Sue's other brother Gary and his wife, Benny, are also staunch supporters of my cause. Benny, too, wept and hugged me, saying how sorry she was. Isn't it odd that everyone but the guilty is sorry for what happened? Benny has, on more than one occasion, talked for hours on end to Sue, and she gets angry too. Cassy, my other sister-in-law, has given me unconditional support. She e-mails articles to me, and she tells me her thoughts on sexual abuse and tries to comfort me. These things amaze me. Maybe you can't understand from the nonvictim side, but I haven't felt worthy of any of this. When you are repeatedly told that even God doesn't love you, you can't get past that easily.

I think there is a big difference between healing and coming to terms. It is a personal wrestling match that I often have with myself. I still have my difficult moments and even days, but Sue is so tuned into me that they pass, with her comforting me.

While I still can't pray, I do speak to God. Sometimes, however, it's more like yelling, from my side. But that, too, is OK. It's not like God can't take it. I believe that he understands how I feel and that he understands the disconnect I feel with him. That is one bridge I can't seem to cross yet. The day will come, but it can't be forced. It will happen, if it is truly meant to be.

I try to look upon every day that I get up as a gift from God. He hasn't taken me in the night, and today I will work toward healing and extending myself to others who are early on in their journey or who are more shaky than I. I am thankful for my wife, children, grandchildren, three of my siblings, and my in-laws. So many broken people whom I meet don't have this kind of support, and that makes it all the more tragic for them. Some, I feel, will only have peace upon leaving this world, but, while it's not my sole mission in life, I try to help those less fortunate than I.

If I can reach but one person in writing this book, then I have succeeded. It was cathartic for me to write this, and it aided in my letting go of some of my pain. However, in the same vein, it is harder to put it in print than to talk or speak about it. Seeing it in words has made me cry, as I look back over it. On the other hand, seeing it in words has made me feel that I am worth something and that I am loved. While I never see myself trusting anyone easily, I do see the strength of the people who love me. And for that, I am thankful.

I hope that reading this book has given you the password into my world, as Dr. Driscoll told me it did for him. It is a dark, evil world that needs to be eradicated. It's all about the children. Do whatever you can to protect them.

The aftermath of the man who harmed so many, Rev. Neary, is amazing. According to his obituary, he served in many parishes, and, now that my story and face have been on the news, I hear of other parishes that he infected during his reign of terror. He had quite a career around central New York. At last count, people had come to me about him from fifteen parishes. I have heard from or spoken to over thirty men and one woman whom he terrorized. The broken people he left in his wake runs the gamut from a policeman turned fireman, a teacher, an editor for a well-known magazine, an attorney who works tirelessly to help other victims, a well-known comedian, a man who is in prison for doing to others what Neary did to him, a marina owner, a corporate officer of a major pump manufacturer, to even a brother and a sister. There are some whose relatives contact me to tell of their brother or son who has turned to street life because he can't cope. Others turn to drugs, alcohol, and even suicide. How truly sad. Some of us "made it OK," but that is only the face you see. It is only what we let you see. We are experts at stuffing our feelings, putting them into a dark emotional crevice within our true self. We are your friends, your neighbors, your family members. Many victims talk to me without detailing their lives, only to thank me for what I do because they can't. Even the bishop told me that I am doing God's work, ministering to those lost sheep.

I am grateful to SNAP too. They have showed me that there is hope here and now, and that as we look to the horizon, maybe, just maybe, we can save some children from the fate that we had to endure. It is a little odd that former Catholics and former priests are the mainstay to try and rid the Church of this evil. One would think that Catholics themselves would be out front leading the charge, and not the victims and so many former Catholics. This is not to say that there are not some terrific Catholics out there, such as the VOTF (Voice of the Faithful), and others, however there are millions of Catholics and only thousands of these same Catholics come forward to try and rid their church of the abusive clergy and very publicly support those of us who have been abused. There are also many active Catholics and active priests that work with and support SNAP. It just pales in comparison to the total number of Catholics who should be demanding their church leadership fix the crisis.

29

WHERE I AM TODAY

Where I am today. That's quite a loaded question. Many years have passed since my tenth birthday. I am getting to the point where I truly believe that I am not guilty. I regret what happened, but now realize that I was powerless to help myself. Too many of my fellow victims can't see that yet. It has been a hard three years in therapy, but I am OK. Ok is a word I used in the past to keep people at bay. I felt that somehow if I answered differently, I would risk contaminating them. The words to describe how I feel are hard to come up with, but I feel like I have never felt before.

I've told Sue and Dr. Driscoll that I feel like I am in uncharted territory. I still look over my shoulder, both emotionally and physically as I am unsure of myself still. It is a little frightening to let go of the feelings from the past; however, that has been the goal all along. What happened, happened. That can't be changed. However, the sting associated with the memories can heal. You can't unremember tragic events of your past. The memories still lie there, just under your personal radar, if you will.

Who would ever think that feeling good about yourself would be scary? We have all heard about the "shoe falling" when something bad happenes to us. We wait for the "other shoe" to drop. The other shoe falling—sometimes though, there is only one shoe, and it has already fallen. I look back over the last forty-plus years and see myself as well on my way to being a survivor. I was a victim, and I began my journey to survivor with a lot of help. I am not finished in my journey, but I can look forward to a good "rest of my life." I have expunged my guilt, my shame, and my embarrassment.

Along my journey to the present, I have found that I have been a perfectionist in school and in work. I trained many people in their jobs, in an effort to exert control, in contrast to my situation as a child, in which I had no control.

At times, I do admit to gazing over my shoulder and seeing the victim behind me, and I look forward to achieving survivor status. With each look back, though, the victim is shrinking in size, while looking forward, I get ever nearer to survivor status.

I am worthy of unconditional love, after all; and I am enjoying it, even savoring it, if you will. I have let go of my fears. Sue remains steadfast at my side, my soul mate, put in my life by God, she feels. My children still love me without reservation, and so do their spouses. Three of my siblings and both my mom and mother-in-law remain at my side. Also, my brothers-in-law (except Jane Doe's husband), and sisters-in-law stand true too. The fear of the unknown also leads to the concealment of your abuse. There is this overwhelming fear that you'll lose everyone once they know. Part of that is true, as a very wise man told me once: "Whoever is left in my life after the dust from this has settled is truly my family." That wise man was Dr. Driscoll.

People remain quick to judge me at times. I would not and am not asking them to leave their Catholic faith. What I do want is for them to get it. My kids (my adult children) get it. Tracy, steadfastly, is at my side with unconditional support, ready to "take out" anyone who would harm me. Jerry compares me to the most precious of stones, a diamond. Lee says that to think of my abuse hurts too much. Chas, while building the Web site for this book, has said that I am his hero.

30

SUE ASKS ABOUT
SHATTERED BELIEFS

By—Susan Currier Bailey

Sue and I in 1997 at our twenty-fifth wedding anniversary. Thankfully, she is still by my side today.

Why are my beliefs shattered? My mother taught me to always see good in everyone, but as an adult, I realize that not all people are good or trustworthy. In a perfect world, what my mother taught would be wonderful, but in the real world, we must see people as they really are. Good people want so badly to trust everyone. We want to believe that others think and feel as we do. We never assume that there are others who are pure evil. Or even very sick-minded. Where do these people come from? What kind of families did they have? And most important, how in the name of God did they end up as priests in the Catholic Church for the past few centuries?

What were the bishops thinking when they just moved these people? They had to know that just relocating the priests wasn't working. It hadn't for years. Did they not care? Victims never talked about their abuse to anyone, not even each other. The church always felt safe because this was such an embarrassing crime that very rarely anyone would speak of it, not even to people they loved and trusted. As long as that remained true, the Church had nothing to worry about. Nothing to worry about—what is wrong with that statement? Why didn't they, as moral leaders, care what was happening to the children? Why were the priests' lives much more important than the children's safety? The church wants to say that the abuse is a society problem that happens everywhere. That makes it worse—when you can't go to your church for help. I always thought that that's what the Church was there for. And when it does happen in society, how many perpetrators get away with it, if the police are called?

"The bishop will handle it." That's just what so many were told. The bishops handled it all right. With no punishment. With no ban against these men ever being around children. No, the priests were able to have more children and no police record. These priests were able to paralyze their next victim with promises of becoming a priest. Then the priests would go on their merry way after the damage was done, as carefree as ever, never worrying, but fully conscious of what they had done. So how can we feel that this is a society problem when the priests broke the law and didn't have to live by the laws that we have in place to protect us?

The bishops should never be called in these matters. The police should arrest these priests, and these priests should stand trial. Let the criminal system work, and let a jury make a decision after all facts are presented. For the Church that claims to be good, where was the good in what happened? Where was the protection? Where was the pain in their hearts for the victims? The victims were children, and the priests were grown men, with way too much authority over the children. Shame on us for giving them that much power over us. Shame on them for demanding it. Where is the church's shame? Are they only apologizing now because they have been caught? Will they continue to hide as much as possible, hoping the real truth will never come out? Not as long as strong, courageous survivors are alive to demand the truth.

31

THIRTY-FOUR YEARS OF MARRIAGE TO A MAN I THOUGHT I KNEW

By—Susan Currier Bailey

I knew Charley inside out. I truly thought that I could finish his every sentence and know his every thought. We are that close. He was and is my very best friend. Our four children love him. His eight grandchildren adore him. When I met Charley, it was not love at first sight. It was for him, but not for me. He is such a good person and a very good friend. You can see after meeting him, the gentleness in his personality. I had no clue about the demons that haunted him. I never guessed the secret that he would hide from me for thirty years. I gave him a small kiss after our first date, and he told me that he felt we would be married some day. I just laughed and smiled at him like he was kidding, but he wasn't. Time went on, and I fell in love with the warmest most sensitive person I know. He became my best friend and soul mate.

When our youngest child, Jerry, told his father that he was having his first child, my husband told him he would make a wonderful father. Jerry said instantly, "I learned from the best." That about sums up Charley. But little did I know the deep, dark secret that he kept from me and from everyone who loved him. The shame and embarrassment he felt, haunted him for years, and he felt that he was alone with his secret. The shame took over, and he buried it deeper and deeper, so he would no longer feel the pain of his childhood. He practiced many times in the mirror, trying to tell me. How could he get the courage? How would I feel about him after I knew? He thought that I would feel disgust—that was his word for what he thought I would feel. Disgust was also what he felt about himself for being a victim of Father Neary. How would his parents or his siblings feel about him if they knew?

Being a child of ten when the abuse occurred, he did not even realize that what he was doing was even sex. He knew that he hated it. He knew that it was the most pain he had ever felt. He also knew that his mother was so very pleased that a priest would grace their home with his presence. Charley has memories of his mother on the phone with all her friends, telling them so proudly that a priest was at her home, paying attention to her son. She would get her priest in the family. Her second-born son. How proud she would be. Charley's emotions were so mixed. He knew that his mother was so happy, and he could not figure out why. Why would she want me to experience such pain and suffering? Maybe that's what Father Neary had told her? Charley, maybe, in his ten-year-old mind, started to believe that the pain and suffering was just what was expected of him in order to become a priest. For Charley to become a priest was his mother's dream, although it was Charley's nightmare.

What did his mother think when Charley begged not to go with the priest? Father Neary would tell her that he was preparing Charley for the priesthood. He told her that he needed alone time with Charley and to keep the other children downstairs as he took Charley upstairs. Charley's sister Carol remembers being told not to go up stairs when Father Neary was with Charley. She could not understand why not, but she did what she was told. Charley's mother was, and still is, such a good Catholic, that her blind faith in such an evil person just because he wore a collar cost her her innocence and the innocence of her fourth child. That is too big of a price to pay. My mother-in-law's name is Mary. She was and is a good mother, and she did everything to protect her children. It's hard for me to believe that she never saw anything or suspected anything out of the ordinary. Or just maybe she did, but she was raised by a strong Catholic mother and a Catholic police officer father, with an aunt who was a nun. If she had not met my father-in-law, she would also have become a nun as she told all of us so many times. Her mind could not believe that a priest would or could ever be capable of such evil actions. After all, priests were like God. How sad a statement that is. No one on this Earth is godlike. Only God can be God. If anything, the Catholic priest abuse scandal has taught us how true that really is. Just because a man puts on a black garment and white collar, he does not deserve total trust.

I will never in my life forget what Charley's mother said when we told her about the abuse. She said that she would have rather heard that someone in the family had died—even one of her own children, rather than to have heard that Charley had been abused by the priest. So really, the news that one of her other children had died would have been better news than Charley's abuse? That makes me have to sit down and wonder how bizarre is that kind of thinking, and what was she taught as a child? How very sad. A statement she made many times to everyone in the family was that her religion was first, then her husband, then her children. That explains so much.

She was taught that a priest for her was a man of God. He was God's messenger. They forgot to tell her that the priest was just like you and me—no better no worse. If she only knew that, she would have never given her child up to his trust so willingly.

So, in her middle eighties, Charley's mother had to deal with how could someone so godlike do something so awful to a child and then threaten him into silence? I'm sure that she felt betrayed, and that she wanted with all her heart to believe that he was the only priest who ever did this. If that were the truth, it would be the end of this story. Unfortunately, Father Neary is one of many, too many. As of today, ten bishops have resigned because of allegations against them. It seems like a nightmare that will not go away to most Catholics, but I say they should thank God every day for all the brave men and women who have come forward and done all they could to remove the priests that were abusers. The average person has no idea how hard and difficult it is for someone to say that they were abused. It definitely was the hardest thing that my husband ever did in his life. If it wasn't for these men and women, the Catholic Church would be far more dangerous than it is today, for the Church never felt a need to clean it up until someone forced them to. They would just help the priests with their little problems and move them to a new parish. It's not all cleaned up. There is still a long way to go, but I see some light. This is the first year that we will have, at our 2006 SNAP convention, a bishop who is also a survivor of sexual abuse. Some nuns attended and talked of all the abuse they have known about. We know we've made a difference when priests, nuns, and bishops attend SNAP Conferences because they are sick of the abuse. That speaks volumes!

Father Neary went on to allegedly molest numerous other young boys and, to our knowledge, he never felt threatened that anyone would do anything to stop him. He felt safe in the haven of the Catholic Church. The Church had no problem protecting him and others who molested children. We know now that the Church never did anything except send some priests to in-house counseling, and then usually they would put them in a new parish with no consideration as to what else they were capable of.

This never worked. The cover-up became more widespread, but the Church got better at hiding it. They sent priests to other dioceses with glowing recommendations, no less. Catholics today deserve better than what happened to my husband. They deserve to be able to trust their priests and to expect that no one in the name of God or otherwise would ever touch and hurt their child. That begins with the release of the names of the molesting priests. All Catholics should demand the names of the abusers from their bishops. Silence is not the answer. The solution is honesty. If you do not demand the names you cannot complain when this happens to a child or grandchild. It's up to you to make your church safe. As long as molesters are protected, how on Earth do we begin to trust any priest with our children, when we have no idea which ones to trust? You can say, "It's not my priest. He presides over our family funerals and family weddings, and is always there for us. He is the police chaplain. He hears our confession and gives us Holy Communion. How could he hold the Holy Eucharist one minute and, the next minute, touch a little child in that way as many victims have told me?"

Good question. The only real answer is that pure evil exists. As long as I'm alive, I will never understand how someone that understands God the way the priests and bishops do can believe in their heart that they will ever see God after being part of the abuse or part of the huge cover-up.

The reason I'm writing this is because of the morals I was taught in Catholic school. Even though I am no longer a Catholic, I learned right and wrong, what God expects from me, and what he expects me not to do.

Canon law prevents one priest from saying anything about another priest, no matter what terrible act they have committed. I have lost count of how many victims certain priests have seen as they entered a room, witnessed what was going on, and did nothing to help. Some priests, when they have seen abuse going on have only said to the offending priest, "Are you at it again?" This has been stated by several victims of clergy abuse. How is it that this church feels the need to protect men like this? Maybe they feel that the poor priest is sick and needs help, never thinking how much help all the children he abused might need. They never thought about how some of the abused children would even take their own lives.

If the offender was your friend or neighbor, and even if you truly liked him, you'd want him hauled off to jail immediately until things were sorted out. So is the moral of the story that if you'd like to molest little girls or little boys and never have any consequences for your behavior, then a priest is what you may want to be? This attitude needs to change. If it were a teacher, or health care worker, or a policeman, or neighbor, or child care worker, they would instantly be removed and placed into custody, pending investigation. I would love to feel differently, but I can't until changes in the Church take place. I've only known of four courageous self-assured priests and former priests, but I'm sure there are more. They all have had their hands slapped and have been reassigned for speaking up. One is A. W. R. Sipe, who spent eighteen years as a Benedictine monk and was trained to deal with the mental health problems of priests and Catholic Church officials. Father Thomas P. Doyle and Patrick Wall are staunch victim supporters. In 1984, Father Doyle became involved with the issue of sexual abuse of children by Catholic clergy. Patrick J. Wall, a former Roman Catholic priest and a former Benedictine monk, has been a senior consultant in Costa Mesa, California, advising on over two hundred cases of sexual abuse relating to the Catholic Church. The last one, Father Robert Hoaston, was a Catholic priest and who was brave enough to speak of his abuse at the Senate hearing. Then shortly after testifying, he was removed from his job. Some priests will actually get into Heaven.

Any priest who talks to his congregation about how these victims only want money knows darn well that that is not true. If the priest says the abuse crisis is over, or that it's only 1 percent of all priests who abuse children, then he is a priest I would never trust. Other priests are still making excuses for the downfall of their priesthood. The priests seem to need to blame the victims instead of the true perpetrators. These priests are truly wolves in sheep's clothing.

The so-called good Catholics believe and say just what they hear in church. Victims want money. Who in their right mind would put themselves through such pain and embarrassment? I said once to my husband, "Are you really ready to be out there in your underwear?" His reply to me was, "Hell, it's more like being naked in front of the world." No one asks for that. If anything, they hide from it. Most of the victims I know are very private people, and they only disclosed the abuse because their abusing priest is still in the ministry. They are horrified that the abuse will happen again.

Our children are not safe. They won't be safe until all the child molesters have been told to remove their collars, and that doesn't look like any time soon. The Church seems to believe that they need to protect these men for the rest of their lives, although it doesn't seem to matter how many lives the priests have ruined or how many of their victims have committed suicide. These priests are the purest of evil, but still they are protected by a church that will always protect them. Pedophiles do not stop. They have a desire for children that just keeps on going. So how can we feel that our children are safe within the Catholic Church? You would have to believe that, because the Pope said "no more," the pedophiles would just quit then. That's something for us to think about. How safe do you feel now? Catholics, as a group, need to get a voice and demand the abusers be laicized and not allow them to simply retire with a medical plan, pension, and maybe even a car and housing. Would you want your coach, teacher, or other person who abused just retire with no consequences? A retired priest, that is a known abuser, is more dangerous, they have all day every day to be with children. Start protecting your children and grandchildren, they are our future and deserve to have a church free of abusers.

I'm writing in my husband's book to help everyone put a face to this horrifying priest abuse. When I first sat down with others abused by priests, I came to understand all the different aspects of clergy abuse. I understand that sexual abuse with clergy not only takes away the victim's innocence, his youth, and the way he trusts, but it also takes God away from him as a young child.

A young victim cannot believe that God wants this, even as he is being told those very words. But, who are you to question a priest, a man of God, and a person whom your parents look up to? You're expected to look up to him too. Many survivors of abuse at the hands of a priest feel paralyzed at the thought of reporting the priest. Priests are like other pedophiles except they have a collar, which makes them more dangerous. After all, who would ever believe a child over a priest?

Many other religions do not understand how the Catholics gave so much power to the priests—how they truly gave them godlike power, not realizing they were merely men. How terribly dangerous. Hopefully, we can get the next generation to realize this and expect their children to be safe—to actually demand that their children are safe. I truly believe that the younger, more educated, generation respects priests, but are smart enough not to trust them. They realize that priests are human like you and I, which means that they are capable of both good and bad behavior.

I sat in my kitchen one day and came to the conclusion that I had always known that the world had its many problems, but I had always thought that I could trust the Church and turn to my faith in God at times of need. Our local bishop, in keeping with new church policy, performed the audit and training on everyone working with children who was involved with the Catholic Church. Even the priests. What a wonderful idea. Everyone felt safe and happy. Except for the people who knew better. Guess what? That is just not good enough; any one with half a brain knows that the priests who have been sent away, even the worst offenders, have no convicted criminal backgrounds to check.

Their criminal records do not exist; they are as clean as Mother Teresa. Why? Because they were *never* turned over to the authorities! So how can the Church be so tolerant of these behaviors and work so hard at flimsy attempts to smooth over the Catholic Church's image? Let's all think as Catholics; they never had to prove what they said was true, we never questioned them, we always believed that what was said was gospel, and therein lies the dangers of blind faith.

Why does the truth scare the daylights out of most Catholics and others, who want the truth but are too afraid to demand it? How could they ever stand up to the priest, and if they did, would he then shun them? How would they ever live with that? I'll tell you something—it would be a lot easier to live with that than to be my mother-in-law, living with the guilt every day of having not seen something she should have seen that was right in front of her face. She loves her son but knows in her heart that she was dead wrong, and she apologizes all the time. Sometimes she calls him up crying, saying that she is sorry and then hangs up. I know that she is truly sorry for not seeing what was in front of her eyes.

2002 was the year she stopped going out to church. After four years, in 2006, she was placed in a nursing home where she started to attend church once again. She remains firm in her faith, which is good. After all it is not the Catholic faith at fault for the clergy abuse crisis, but rather some of the priests and bishops in the church. She watches church services on TV but does not attend services at a church unless her daughter, "Jane Doe," insists. It's so sad that at her age of eighty-eight, she has to realize the pure evil that exists in the Catholic Church. She still loves her church, and that will not change, nor should it near the end of her life. She has truly asked for forgiveness from my husband for not protecting him. And that helps Charley in his quest for healing.

When I looked into one woman's eyes on a cold, blustery, winter day a short time ago, I knew there was something I had to include in this book. We were standing outside a courthouse where three other women were filing a lawsuit against the same priest who had also raped her. I could have only respect for her presence there, in the background, quietly not saying a word. She could not come forth when they filed her lawsuit because of the pain and discomfort it caused, to even think about it now. But, because of her courage, others are coming forward and making this priest accountable for his actions.

It did not take away the feeling of embarrassment that the priest had made her feel many times. It did not take away the horrified feeling of ever seeing him again, but she stood there, brave and anxious to see some justice done. She did not have to say a word, with her husband by her side. You could see that he loved and supported her. She had a hat covering her hair, and her eyes were the most bloodshot eyes I've seen in a long time. The sadness showed all over her face. I wanted to hug her and tell her it would be OK. But I knew not to, for she did not know me, and I did not want to make her more uncomfortable than she already was. I also wanted to say that that priest would suffer because of all the young girls he abused, but truthfully none of us are sure of that. She is a mother of seven children, and she homeschooled them for a while. Like many victims of sexual abuse, she never wanted her children to feel the pain of the abuse she had felt.

There was no makeup on her eyes. She told me that it's very hard to want to look beautiful when you've been raped so young. She never wanted that sort of attention ever again. She did not want her name used here, because she was protecting her children.

People can be ignorant and rude, and she did not want what happened to her to affect her children. The victims are starting to come forward in such great masses. It has always been about children and keeping them safe. The priest who molested ten years ago, twenty years ago, thirty, forty, or even fifty years ago, is still a molester. He could still be out there, and he just may be your parish priest.

How does that make us feel safe? The church will never make the priests' names public. I can't say that enough. That's why it's up to survivors of clergy abuse to come forward and help remove these monsters. There are many reasons why victims of clergy abuse do not come forward. Following disclosure, many victims lose some of the closest people in their lives—siblings, friends, co-workers, neighbors, relatives, even parents. Some people just can't or won't understand how this kind of abuse could happen. Reality becomes like a nightmare, and they wish they could wake up and go back to believing that someone like a priest could never do such a thing.

So, in some cases, the victims are told by the Church and family to *get over it. It happened a long time ago. Just forgive the priest.* How, in the name of God, do you forgive a priest still in active ministry who is still a very clear danger to children? The Church says that they want their happy little family back, with no consideration as to what the victim had to go through just by revealing this after so many years. My husband always says that we can't just forget that pedophile priests exist. Forgetting it is like trying to unring a bell. Once it's rung, there's no looking back. The sacrifice of family members who do not understand makes you realize who really and honestly loves and cares for you. We were very blessed to have four children and their spouses who support what we do to stop this abuse and know that what we do is the right thing.

The survivors we have come to know very well now have become like members of our family. Very strong bonds form, and we say how blessed we are to have them in our lives. People ask all the time how if you kept this secret for so long, why do you now have to talk about it? I say, why not now? If only they felt whole enough and not so beaten down about going up against the Catholic Church, then maybe a good question would be "how many children could have been saved if we had talked sooner?" But really, until the brave *Boston Globe* brought most of this into the public eye, most survivors felt alone with their dirty secret. If those compassionate, wonderful writers didn't feel that something was so dead wrong, then the story would never have been told. The stories of abuse, the cover-up, and the relocation of priests so they would never be punished would never have been looked at by anyone. Even though I believe that abuse is still happening even as you sit and read this, the Church will only become better at covering up. It's up to us, all of us, to police where our children go and with whom and never assume that, if they are with a priest, that it is safe. Where in the Bible does God want us to close our minds and hearts to a problem?

One victim said to me, "I'm not leaving the Church." The priests who abuse children are leaving, not me. The priest that abused her is still practicing within a nice big church. The Church does not get it. We need to remember that the priests who abuse are seen as wonderful men, men you would love to invite for dinner. It is the nature of predators to cultivate loyalty. They always make sure that they are well liked and even loved by all the family members. They become beyond reproach.

I don't know of any abuse case involving a priest where the victim did not say their mom or dad had just loved the priest. How calculating is that? If the priest were a shady character, no one would have trusted his or her child with him. So what's a good Catholic to do? Well, many feel that praying will do the trick! Some Catholics think they can pray it away. If we just pray a little bit harder, the priest will no longer abuse and the victims will heal and all this will stop. In real life, the victims want nothing more than to heal and feel whole again. It feels so awful to feel burdened with this pain. I truly believe that the Catholic Church loves the fact that a lot of Catholics feel they can pray it away. As long as that's your answer to the crisis in the Church, nothing will ever change. Another one of my husband's quotes is, "It's OK to pray, but you still need to row your boat for shore." Something my husband wants more than anything else is to not to be a victim. He says that when this kind of abuse has happened to you, then, even if you're in a room with no one you know, you still feel like the other people in the room somehow know of your past. It's something that he will carry around with him for the rest of his life.

Who does the abuse affect? It affects one victim and also his or her children, grandchildren, his or her spouse, a mother and a father, brothers and sisters, aunts and uncles, cousins, friends, co-workers, and neighbors. People you deal with every day now have to face that it happened. They have to figure out where you now fit into and, in some cases, do not fit into their lives.

Some of these people believe, truly believe, that a priest did this horrible act to you. Others can't even imagine that that wonderful priest could have done such a horrifying act. They would rather believe it was a child's fault than a priest's fault. They actually think that the child wanted sex, and he or she led the priest on, never considering for one minute what that sounds like. If they were not talking about a priest, they would stop those kinds of excuses immediately. Why does the abuse happen? Because it could happen. There was no one and nothing to stop it. The church had more power than anyone knew. There were so many years of abuse that no one knew how to stop it. Many tried by getting the police involved, only to be told that it was a church matter. What arrogance—how dare the police not do the right thing in protecting our children? Some of the victims are still Catholic. But some do not even believe in God anymore. Some have tried like hell to get back into the Church, only to be so abused again. Abuse in the name of religion is so very hard to grasp. Our four children support what we do, educating and speaking to groups about clergy abuse. We have been very blessed that they and their spouses all love us unconditionally.

Some people wonder how in the world this abuse could have happened. It happened because the Church did not put the interest of children first. The priests' well-being always came first, and it still does today. What happened to "Do what Jesus would do"? One alleged priest had the audacity to hire two private investigators to try to find dirt on one woman who had accused him of rape when she was underage. Then, other victims came forward after the first woman did. But the priest still feels guiltless. He does not feel like he did anything wrong. It's almost like the abusive priests feel that they are entitled to abuse children. A very interesting thing about that is that some priests who claim they are celibate, believe they are celibate as long as they do not have sex with adult women. They think that having sex with a child, boy or girl, or with a man, does not break their vow of celibacy. That in and of itself is the most dishonest thing I have ever heard. Who do they think they are, making such horrid rules for themselves?

All Catholics should be outraged with the excuses and dishonesty from the Catholic Church and the cover-ups that still exist. They should be outraged, not knowing who has done these despicable things to children. Where is the outrage? You all need outrage, or you will be in danger that this will happen again and again—to your children or to your grand children.

Barbara Blaine, president of SNAP (Survivors Network of those Abused by Priests) said, at a conference in Denver, that no one will be coming to your door to thank you because their child did not get abused by a priest, but by exposing these priests and demanding them out of their parishes, we may help children to not be abused. There are no thanks for that—only inner peace.

Many of us live and die without really touching the lives of others, especially if they are not part of our immediate families. We become very selfish in believing that we can just exist without caring for our neighbors. We have become preoccupied with our families, and so we do not care about what happens to others. We have a wonderful man named Phil who comes to our SNAP group. He is there because he could not sit back and watch a man he knew as a child suffer the long-term effects of priest abuse alone. He said that he walked by the TV and saw this man John being wheeled out of the courthouse, and he said to himself, "Get off your ass and help this man." How many of us would have just sat back and said "that's too bad, I wish I could help," and never do a thing about it, or "maybe I'll just pray for that man." Not good enough!

Phil did the praying and more. He stepped up to the plate, took things a step forward, and he became someone who is so admired, because this is not a family member or someone he has to care about, but he still cares. He could not sit back and see John suffer alone anymore. He became a true friend in every sense of the word and he became far more to all the survivors. He has given money out of his own pocket to help survivors. He has paid for those who could not afford to attend seminars, and he speaks with the bishop about removing priests who have been accused of child molestation. You might ask where he came from. Is he too good to be true? What is his motive? His motive is clear. He is one of the most compassionate, sympathetic persons you'll ever meet. When survivors speak, you can look over at Phil, and his eyes will be red because he hurts for others. If we all felt like Phil, the world would be a better place. What a wonderful world it would be.

A couple of summers ago, I realized that four adult children of a local Catholic family had committed suicide. How odd that they were all from one family, and no one had said what happened there. What had caused so many in one family to do such a thing? A better question is why? What caused this to happen? What did they all have in common that they took their lives? Many of us want to say that maybe it was too many bills or not enough love—who really knows except them, and they cannot tell us now? We need to listen to what we do not want to hear when someone says that a certain priest is a child predator, no matter how nice you happen to feel he is, and I'm sure you do feel that way. We need to pay attention to all the signs. How big do you need the sign to be? You do not want to become like my mother-in-law, who feels so much guilt over what she failed to prevent. Signs were there, but she chose not to see them. Why? Because he was a priest, a man of God. He could not be doing anything wrong. How could he? How could she believe that anything was wrong? Even if her child cried to not go with him, she needed that priest to be involved with the family.

Your child or grandchild is not worth sacrificing for the sake of a priest. We all must remember that priests are only people, just like you and I—no better no worse. We need to listen to all allegations made about clergy like we would if it were anyone else. Stop defending them, because they wear a collar. I guarantee if you do not remove them that could be your child next. It's better to err on the side of caution for our children, than to assume that a person who is accusing a priest is wrong. It is not worth damaging the child's innocence. You can never give that back, no matter how hard you try. It is something that all children of child molestation want back—their innocence. Today, we all have a very good idea of who the predators are. There are Web sites to track, and we can read the papers and view TV news to get a good idea of whom we should not trust. We all know the people who will not look or accept that this crisis is happening. I want to call these people the pod people or "sheeples," the sheep people. Thank God that they are few and far between. Many, many Catholics are now getting on board and asking what they can do to help. The behavior of the Church is no longer acceptable to them. One of our courageous mothers, a SNAP leader whose sons were abused, was asked to sign a statement saying that the priest did not act outside of normal standards. She now knows, sadly, that it was probably right. These appear to have been the Church's normal standards back then. She and her sons stood strong, and, even though they could have used the money offered because she was divorced with four children, they refused to sign. The Church settled with the family for far less money, but at least they did not have to sign a lie, a gag order. The signs of abuse are there, but everyone is scared to death to ask the questions, much less hear the answers. It may be too hard to fix, or it just may be too hard to handle. It almost seems like the victims are all little ants, and they're trying so very hard to survive. Some of them are stamped out almost before they start. Those are the many victims who have committed suicide. Others run for their lives.

Those are the victims who know that the abuse is dead wrong but cannot find their voices. They feel ashamed for what had happened to them, and I truly understand that. The strongest get through everything, even through the struggle. They can fight for survival. I can only hope that all survivors will feel that power—the power to change things and to make sure that this is the end of clergy abuse as we know it. The victims who have committed suicide are like the dead ants; even if they die, some of their families still feel attacked by the other ants as the victim is carried off. Even if the ant dies, it is still under attack by the others. The Church just wants the survivors to go away. The Church never dreamed that they would ever have to deal with this so-called problem. One thing the Church used to be sure of was that not one victim would stand up against the whole Catholic Church. Victims and their families never took their complaints past the Church, especially when it was always said that the Church would take care of the problem. The families and victims would hope that the priests would never be near other children and that they would go straight into counseling. No one would need to know, and the Church could help the family in many ways, even with money to help the child. Every good Catholic believed every word that they were told by the Church—why wouldn't they? A lot of priests who already had counseling were just moved into another parish and told to be good. After all, this was getting to be more and more expensive. I think that the Church worried far more about the money than the children. No one except the victim knows how it is to be raped by a priest in the name of God. Then the victim finds out that this priest went on and on and on raping others with nothing to stop him from his deviant behavior. After all, it was known by the bishops, and even the Pope, and nothing was really happening to any one of them. If I were a man and a pedophile, I would run, not walk, to become a priest, as historically, the priesthood has been a safe haven for pedophiles. But today is a new day, and some very courageous men and women have found their voices. They say that this happened to them and that they are not going to take it any longer! Others tell the people who do stand up, that it happened to them, too, but they can't tell anyone else. They are all in different places, and some that I thought would never do something as small as writing a letter to the editor and signing his or her name, have done so, with the support and love that SNAP gives to them. It's so wonderful when they can find their voices.

This does scare the Church; remember, for centuries no one ever spoke of this. It became the Church's dirty little secret. Most clergy in the Church knew of this, but no one talked of it. Pain and suffering is something easily inflicted on a victim. Then, when he or she is not believed, it's so easy for the Catholic Church to say that they instead believe their parish priest. The members of the Church have a hard time believing that their priest did anything that was so unholy and so unlike God.

Giving the priests so much power and believing they are godlike, I believe is such a sin in and of itself. A bishop stated to me, "Who told you to give a priest so much power? We didn't teach you that. They are like you and me. No better, no worse." However, I attended Catholic schools, and every thing we were taught was to give priests that power. When they came into a room, we stood, and we greeted them with a name that isn't worthy for anyone other than our own fathers. We confessed to them the sins that we told no one else about. Then we wonder why, when a small child is asked to perform a sexual act with the priest, he does not know the right way to react. My own husband really felt that his mother would wash his mouth out with soap if he ever told her that a priest did anything bad to him. He was scared to death of the priest and equally scared of what his mother would do. After all, every time Father Neary came to the house to rape him, the priest would tell his mother that she was going to get the priest she had always wanted. That gave such mixed emotions to a little ten-year-old boy who had no idea that what the priest was doing was sex.

If you think about it—no one wants that kind of media attention after disclosure, for any amount of money. Someone like my husband, by going public, took such a chance. He did not know how our four children would handle it, and the bigger question was how would the son-in-law and daughters-in-law handle it? Would they trust our grandchildren with my husband, because we all know the excuses that so many child molesters use? Molesters can say, "It happened to me as a child," and the public says, "Aw, then you couldn't help yourself." Bull****. My husband always says that life is full of choices. You choose to be evil and inflict the pain that was inflicted on you, or you choose to be determined never to let anyone feel the pain of the abuse that you suffered. It's very interesting that the bishop said some of the priests used that same excuse for their disgusting behavior. My husband used to believe that Father Neary was the one and only priest who ever abused children. He felt that our children were safe at a Catholic high school. Out of four children, only our oldest is still Catholic, and he recently told me that he rarely attends church.

Who is Charles Bailey? A man of integrity. A man who has a definite feeling for what is right and wrong. He is strong enough to stand up for what is right, even if it causes pain and suffering in his own life. He is and always will be a man I am proud to call my husband. Not every one can say that with honesty. He says that what he wants most in his life is his childhood back. To be happy, just like all children should be. He was robbed of this. He would also like his nightmares to end, or at least lessen. He wants to be able to close his eyes and not see this monster who terrorized him for years. But he can never have that, for, you see, he is a survivor of priest abuse. Still, he chooses to make a difference in his own life and lives of others. Because of this, he is my hero and a hero to countless others. He has absolutely made a difference in the world we live in.

Many survivors are coming forward, and they are all brave heroes. In fact, they are some of the most courageous, wonderful people I have ever met. My husband is a local SNAP leader, and he talks to local and out-of-town groups like Voice of the Faithful and Call To Action. He has educated them on how to help and treat the survivors of clergy abuse.

For the last thirty-four years, my husband never allowed anyone too close. His oldest brother, Bill, always called him the angry American. He had a few friends that he felt he could trust, but he trusted no one with his secret. I think that he always felt that if somebody got too close, then he or she might see his shame, and that was something he worked so hard, for so long, to keep to himself. That was his pain, and he never wanted any one of his friends or family to feel the pain and disgust that he felt every day. So he kept his secret, and he put it away—so far away that it only crept up on him in his nightmares and in the quiet times that most of us enjoy. He hated quiet times because they only reminded him of the evil times he had in his life, so he kept our lives busy and jumping. He wanted his four children and later his eight grandchildren around all the time. I would be so totally worn out, and he'd be looking for more commotion. When we first married, he wanted eight children. I put a halt to that. But he now has eight grandchildren, and they are wonderful, each and every one of them. His eyes light up when they walk into the room. He gets his childhood back when he sees their innocence and their freedom to express themselves—things that he never had and could only dream of. Watching the children is the one thing that truly makes him happy.

A dream of being as happy as these eight children puts a smile on his face and laughter in his voice, as they play and run around the house, looking to pick on or play a joke on one another. I'm pulling my hair out, and he's just smiling. I think our children think he's a saint because he is so patient with the grandchildren, but he is just enjoying everything about them, even their spats with each other. To be ten again and to stop this evil priest is something he can only dream about. If only he were not so religious and hadn't believed that this man was God's messenger on Earth, maybe he would have been spared so much pain. Who knows what my husband could have been if he hadn't felt so unworthy his whole life. But I want to tell him that he's so much more. He's my hero, my soul mate, and someone I am so very proud of. Even if I could, I wouldn't change a thing about him.

32

THE FINAL CHAPTER:
DEATH OF
AN ALLEGED ABUSER

This is the final chapter of an alleged sexual predator, Thomas Neary.

He died in September of 2001 at eighty-three years of age. He was educated at both St. Andrews Seminary and St. Bernard's Seminary. He was a Roman Catholic Priest with the Diocese of Syracuse, New York.

Here is a partial list of the churches he was at:

Associate priest at St. Michael's on Onondaga Hill

St. Mary's in Skaneateles

Pastor (a promotion?) at Our Lady Rosary in Hannibal

St. Patrick's in Jordan

Most Holy Rosary in Syracuse

He retired from Most Holy Rosary in Syracuse. A priest at that church told Sue that she was not the first person to complain about Neary to him. That means his career as a child abuser extended forty-years plus.

Others have come to me saying he was also at these parishes from time to time:

Fulton

Norwich

Oswego

New Hartford

Durhamville

Cortland

My journey started with blindfolds on, as that was the only way to protect myself. However, now that they are off, I see the evil very clearly.

When I have been at speaking engagements, I am no longer surprised when people approach me, saying that Neary raped them too. Our local bishop also said I was not the first to come to him about Neary. Sometimes, victims tell me that more than one family member was abused by him.

During one of my visits to the bishop, he went out into the hall from his office and looked up where Neary was buried. He suggested that I go there, so Sue and I drove. I was nervous and anxious at the same time. I had to do this for a sense of closure. He was finally gone.

All I felt was relief that "not one more child" would be damaged by this man. His reign of terror was truly over, and he now had to answer to God for what he did in God's name. I also believed that the others who covered up his trail will have to stand before God and account for their actions. As I knelt over the head-stone, I didn't want to spit on it, as I thought I might. Instead, I felt relief that he was dead. Touching the stone, I felt the evil emanating up through it. It sent a chill up my spine. I never intend to go back.

Dear God … are you there? Hello, hello … this is Charles asking.

I have one final word: When you have looked pure evil in the eye, you are forever changed—forever.

APPENDIX A

FRIENDS AND
FAMILY COMMENT

Please take a moment and visit my Web site at www.intheshadowofthecross.NET (not .com).

On the site is a Family and Friends option. Click on that and you will see how my family and friends feel toward me. Listed below are the ones available at print time. There may be more by now. They are very humbling statements. I am still working with my doctor to be able to see myself as others see me; I have a hard time seeing what they see. The order listed is simply the order in which they were received.

Chuck has impacted my life in more ways than I can count. He is my younger brother. I have watched him grow up from an innocent child to a man who stands tall. When we were growing up I remember the "visits" from the family priest and even though I was only thirteen at the time I felt they were strange. The priest would come and go upstairs for privacy to "teach" him the ways of a priest. I felt that this was strange and voiced this to my parents who thought it was just sibling rivalry. Once I crept up the stairs and sat on the top landing hoping to hear what was so secretive. Now I cannot believe I was so naive. My instinct and heart told me something was wrong but I failed my brother and did not act on it. I noticed a change in him as he became very quiet and solemn. He no longer had an easy laugh and smile on his face. I feel such guilt over this.

Chuck is one of the greatest persons I have ever known. I love him with all my heart. He has made everyone's lives a little better by being there for all of us whenever we needed him. When life has given him blows he has taken them and turned them into strengths instead of weakness. I have seen him over things that would have destroyed someone else and come out the other end the same loving person he is. He makes me proud to call him my brother. One of the biggest regrets of my life is how I let him down by not being there when he needed me the most. It was up to me as his Big Sister to protect and care for him and I failed. *In the Shadow of the Cross* should be read by everyone to see and understand what a child goes through and what strength and perseverance is needed to come through this a whole person. The story of my brother is so heart wretching and painful that it should be a must to read. This book was painful for him to write and painful for his family to watch him relive what had happened. It took much courage and strength of which he has a never-ending well to pull from. Chuck, I love you with all my heart and am proud of what you have done with pouring open your heart and exposing it so others may learn and grow.

All my love,
Carol T Bailey

My Father is Charles L. Bailey Jr. He is very special to me. To know my dad, is to love, honor and respect him. My father has two sides to him; he's an influential man, strong, intelligent and a leader. He's also kind, gentle, understanding, loving, compassionate, considerate and thoughtful everything that you need to be the utmost role model and father figure. My goal in life is to become like him, he is a devoted father, truly dedicated to raising his family.

I am now realizing that some things that were important in life when I was young are not as important now. As I grow older, my dad is teaching me, to be more understanding of others, to try and forgive others, be mindful of other people's feelings and thoughts, to listen more than speak, as you might learn something that you may not have heard otherwise.

When my Father sat me down and first told me about what had happened. I wanted to cry, but with me, instead of depression I filled with anger and hate. My mind doesn't ever rest much, so I thought about it more often than I wanted to. This was very difficult for me to deal with, someone that I love so much, hurting inside. I can't image being him; I know I wouldn't have been as strong as him. I would have lashed out, hurting others (Priests). Then I wouldn't have been the person I am today, with a Beautiful wife and two children. I used to believe that I was a very strong person physically and emotionally, but not even close to my Father. He is the real "Man of Steel" dealing with what life dealt him, and then turning to help others. He is a real life Hero. I am ever so Proud and blessed to have him for a Father. This world would be a much better place if others had a Father like I did.

I love you, Dad …

His son,
Charles L. Bailey III

My dad is special to me. Like many fathers are special to their sons. But mine is different. I have one that worked hard to get to know me and spend time with me. Even when things weren't all that easy to talk about. He always made the effort to let me know that I could talk to him about anything. I know now why that was harder for him than most fathers. I trust him, and that builds a great friendship and understanding. He is one in a million. And for that I am lucky. Like stars in the sky there is one that shines brightest, I call him Dad.

Love, **Jerry**

There are so many words that describe my Dad.… loving, gentle, giving, warm, sensitive, honorable, brave, strong … the list could go on for days. I have to say, hands down, my favorite word to describe my dad is MINE! I am not sure what I did to deserve such an extraordinary man to be my father but I don't question it. I am just thankful everyday that I was blessed with him. I am not the only lucky one though.… my children are too. I don't think there is anyone in this entire world that could compare to him in their eyes.… probably not even me! They adore their "Papa." When I see him with my kids it melts my heart. When I think of all the hurt, pain, confusion and horrific things my dad has gone through in his life, I hurt all over. My heart actually aches for him. There are so many awful paths his life could have gone down but with his incredible strength he chose a path of love and greatness. My dad has asked, "Why did God let this happen to me?" I have pondered that question myself over and over again. The answer that came to me was, God didn't let those things happen to him. God is not a magical God, therefore he cannot control what humans do on earth. He can however take tragedy and show his grace through the strength he gives to victims of tragedy. I believe the Lord has given him that strength to overcome the evil my Dad has endured and in turn also gave him the power to reach out and make a difference in the lives of other victims. I do also believe that God is a just God and Father Neary is now paying for his sins eternally in Hell. It may not be very Christian of me BUT … that thought makes me happy and gives me some peace at night. I cannot even begin to say how proud I am of my Dad. Becoming the head of SNAP in Syracuse, speaking at conferences, fighting to change laws and opening his home to help other victims in despair. Never concerned that most of his free time is devoted to helping others. How could anyone not be in awe of this extraordinary man?

Dad, I love you with all my heart and soul. It is an honor to call you MY Dad.
Tracy

<u>Tracy's and Ty's Children</u> (All they know is grandpa is writing a book and saw their mom writing and wanted to be included)

My grandpa is very helpful and nice. He is the very best grandpa ever. Whenever I'm sad he cheers me up. When I fix stuff with him I feel happy.
Noah's writing

Grandpa has done a lot for me. He is very helpful and whenever something happens he is always there for you and never let's you down. He loves to help and grandpa is a good fixer. He could fix anything. I love my grandpa. He is a very sweet man. I am happy he is my grandpa.
Mariah's writing

My grandfather Charles means so much to me. He has taught me so many things I still use today. He's the reason I pay attention in school, he taught me to do that. He has taught me too many things to be written on paper. I love him so much. He's my favorite grandfather. I love him.
Tyler's writing

In 1990 I met the most beautiful young woman I had ever seen. Shortly after that we began dating and she invited me to meet her family. I'll never forget walking through the front door their home and being greeted by a very tall and intimidating gentleman. I can remember thinking to myself that I better never do anything to make this man angry. He turned out to be the complete opposite of my first impression of him. Three years later I became his son-in-law. Almost immediately after I met him he became a father to me. Any words of wisdom I may have needed or comfort I was seeking, he gave to me as if I was his own flesh and blood. It is impossible to put into words everything he has done for me over the years. Anyone who knows him would tell the same story. None of us ever knew of the demons that chased him every waking moment and into his dreams. He protected all of us from it. That was his job—to protect us from all of the bad things in this world, and show us how much he loved all of us.
Three years ago I began chasing my own demons. In doing so, I shut him out of my life. I caused him great pain when he was already dealing with more than any man should have to. I did this for three long years. When I finally got my life straightened out, I asked him for forgiveness. He didn't even hesitate. He forgave me. That's what a father does for his children. I love you Dad, more than I could possibly put into words. You are my hero. You always have been.

Ty

APPENDIX B

COLLATERAL DAMAGE DONE BY SEXUAL ABUSE

This chart symbolizes with one victim, how many are affected by sexual abuse
Some emotions are good, some bad, there is a mixture of emotions

Charles L. Bailey, Jr.
|

My Mom   My Mother-in-law   My Wife
  My Brother   My Brother-in-law |
  My Sister-in-law My Brother-in-law   Son
  My Sister   My Sister-in-law   Daughter-in-law
  My Brother-in-law   My Grandson
  My Sister   My Granddaughter
  My Brother   Daughter-in-law's Mother
              Daughter-in-law's Father
              |
              Daughter
              Son-in-law
  Relatives   My Grandson
              My Granddaughter
  Co-workers   My Grandson
              Son-in-law's Mother
  Close Friends   Son-in-law's Father
              |
              Son
              Daughter-in-law
              My Grandson
              My Granddaughter
              Daughter-in-law's Mother
              Daughter-in-law's Father
              Daughter-in-law's maternal
                Grandfather
              Daughter-in-law's maternal
                Grandmother
              |
              Son
              Daughter-in-law
              My Granddaughter
              Daughter-in-law's Mother

173

The list goes on and on. No wonder sex abuse is the best kept secret in the world. No one that has been abused wants to hurt so many people.

APPENDIX C

ARTICLES ABOUT THE AUTHOR—REPRINTED WITH PERMISSION

**AFTER YEARS OF SILENCE, MAN TELLS OF ABUSE
HE AND OTHERS URGE ABOLITION OF STATUTE OF LIMITATIONS ON SEXUAL ABUSE BY CLERGY.**

The Post-Standard
Wednesday, *May 21*, 2003
EDITION: Final SECTION: Local PAGE: B1 LENGTH:

BYLINE: By *Erik Kriss* Albany bureau
For decades, Charles Bailey says he kept the secret to himself. After time, the Baldwinsville man admitted it to his wife.

Tuesday, he went public with a story of how he allegedly was abused by a Catholic priest as a boy.

Bailey's voice cracked and he was on the verge of tears as he detailed his journey to Sen. Thomas Duane and others at a public hearing in Albany.

Bailey and other victims, including several from Central New York, implored Duane and his colleagues to pass a law abolishing the statute of limitations for prosecuting clergy sex abuse crimes.

Bailey, now a 52-year-old grandfather of six, said he was abused between the ages of 10 and 12 by a priest in the Syracuse Diocese who has since died. As a teenager, Bailey said, he wanted no one to know. He got married at 21.

"I couldn't tell my young bride of this as I felt so dirty, used and defective," he said. "The shame, guilt and embarrassment was monumental. I would practice telling my wife in the mirror but never could get the courage up."

Plus, he said, they were busy raising their four children.

"I vowed to myself to take it to my grave, as that was the only control I felt I really had," Bailey said. "But with the much-publicized Boston priest abuse, I broke down one day while watching it on TV and told my wife."

Susan Bailey knelt by her husband's side in the Albany hearing room Tuesday and comforted him as he struggled to finish his story.

"I have felt like damaged goods," he said, his voice quavering, "for over 40 years now and it eats me up, every day."

Danielle Cummings, communications director for the Syracuse Diocese, was unable to reach officials Tuesday who could comment.

Charles Bailey called priest sexual abuse "evil" and called the perpetrators "premeditating with their prey. They befriend us, then spend time with us, then meet our families, then befriend our families, all the while laying their groundwork for the planned sexual abuse and rape of us."

Bailey said after the hearing that he decided to go public because his oldest grandson, whom he described as "so trusting and innocent," is about the age he was when he was abused.

"This has got to stop," Bailey said. "We can't have the church hide behind canon law."

Duane, D-Manhattan, has introduced a package of bills that would require clergy to report to police accusations of child abuse going back a half-century; allow adults who believe they were victimized as children more time to sue; and prohibit the use of charitable money for settlements of lawsuits in which the victim must agree to keep the incident secret.

Duane is in the Senate minority and has little ability to get his legislation passed.

But two majority-party lawmakers have introduced clergy-reporting legislation, although it is less far-reaching than Duane's.

Bills sponsored by Sen. Stephen Saland, R-Poughkeepsie, and Assemblyman John McEneny, D-Albany, would require clergy to report child abuse in a family setting to the state's hot line—except allegations learned through confidential communications to clergy that are privileged—and require clergy to search institutional records and report allegations of child abuse by active clergy no matter how long ago. For retired clergy, the church would have to go back 20 years.

Also at Duane's hearing Tuesday, Joyce Nebush, of Utica, head of the Syracuse-Utica chapter of the Survivors Network of those Abused by Priests, told her story of abuse as a child in Massachusetts.

EXTEND *SEX-ABUSE* STATUTE OF LIMITATIONS

The Post-Standard
Sunday, *June 1*, 2003
EDITION: Final SECTION: Opinion PAGE: C2 LENGTH:
TYPE: EDITORIAL

For 40 years, Charles Bailey "felt so dirty, used and defective." As a child, the Baldwinsville man was abused by a priest. He finally came to terms with what happened and testified in Albany about his suffering.

"I have felt like damaged goods," he said, quavering, "for over 40 years now and it eats me up, every day."

Sex abuse is unlike any other crime. Its psychological effects prevent victims seeking justice in a timely way. That is why legislators should change New York's statute of limitations. New York law allows criminal charges filed within three years of a child victim's 18th birthday and civil charges within eight years.

A bill sponsored by state Sen. Thomas K. Duane, D-Manhattan, would allow criminal charges filed until a victim turns 26 or within three years of discovery of the abuse. Many states already have lengthened *sex-abuse* statutes of limitations, as more is known about this horrible crime. The abuse allegations about priests brought the issue to the fore. But the same statute should apply to all victims and their abusers.

Duane's bill stands little chance since he's a Democrat in the Republican Senate. Few of his colleagues showed up at the hearing where Bailey recounted his suffering. Duane's package of bills does single out religious professionals in one appropriate way. He seeks to add clergy members to the list of mandatory reporters of suspected abuse—just as teachers, social workers, police officers and others already are. Bills passed in both houses to do that were never reconciled.

ACCUSER CALLS REPORT A "BABY STEP"
BALDWINSVILLE MAN SAYS TALKING ABOUT HIS ABUSE IS
PAINFUL BUT CATHARTIC.

The Post-Standard
Wednesday, *January 7*, 2004
EDITION: Final SECTION: News PAGE: A10 LENGTH:

BYLINE: By Renee K. *Gadoua* Staff writer

A man who says a priest sexually abused him 40 years ago considers this week's disclosure "a baby step" and calls on the Catholic Church to release the names of all priests guilty of molesting minors.

"It's like saying one of your relatives sexually abused, but I'm not going to tell you who," Charles Bailey said Tuesday. "You should trust your family, but you can't really do it."

Bailey, 52, said memories of abuse by the Rev. Thomas Neary haunt him 40 years later.

Neary died Sept. 17, 2001. Diocesan officials have refused to discuss allegations against him, but offered counseling to Bailey.

"I have nightmares that would keep Stephen King awake," Bailey said during an interview in his Baldwinsville home. A portrait of his four grown children and six grandchildren hung on the wall behind him, and a Christmas tree twinkled in the next room. Sue Bailey, his wife of more than 30 years, sat across the table, frequently stroking his arm as he talked.

"I can tell you what I was wearing," Bailey said of one incident. "It was a two-tone blue shirt and I had the khaki pants on."

At the time of the alleged abuse, Bailey said he was about 10, and Neary was assistant pastor at St. Michael Church, Onondaga Hill. Neary also served at parishes in New Hartford, Skaneateles, Hannibal, Durhamville, Norwich and Jordan, according to the Syracuse Diocese. He was named senior priest in residence at Most Holy Rosary, Syracuse, in 1986 and retired in 1995.

Diocesan officials confirmed Bailey reported the abuse in March.

"I wish to offer my profound apologies for any hurt you have suffered as a result of the despicable activities of one of our priests a number of years ago," Bishop James Moynihan said in an April 2 letter to Bailey. "I know that words are cheap, but what else can I do but apologize and pray for your healing."

Bailey said the diocese has paid about $3,000 in counseling bills.

Bailey said Neary raped him at least 100 times over two years in the early 1960s. He first told his story publicly during a May hearing in Albany calling on state legislators to extend the statute of limitations for prosecuting clergy sex abuse crimes.

Since reporting the abuse, he has been in counseling. He and his wife are co-leaders of the local chapter of the victims' support group Survivors Network of Those Abused by Priests.

Talking about the abuse is painful, but cathartic, he said. And the details never stray from his mind.

"He would come to me in his full garb and abuse me upstairs in my own bedroom," Bailey said, wiping away tears. "He would say he was doing God's will. He would say the Our Father while he was raping me."

Bailey said Neary warned him not to tell anyone.

"He said, 'This is between you and me and God, and if you tell your parents, I'll take them from you,'" he recalled. "At 10, of course I believed him."

Bailey said he has met three times with Moynihan seeking spiritual healing. Moynihan has declined to discuss his meetings with Bailey.

"I feel distance between myself and God," Bailey said. "I need to get right with God. He (Moynihan) was very little help in that area."

He said he shared details with Moynihan, but he's not confident church officials understand the pain and shame victims experience.

"They like to use those fancy words. They don't like to say "raped,'" he said. "They say "misdeed,' 'inappropriate touching,' "mistake.' That's insulting. I'm not a mistake."

ELDERLY OFTEN SILENT ABOUT LONG-AGO CLERICAL ABUSE

The Post-Standard
Friday, *January 9*, 2004
EDITION: Final SECTION: Local PAGE: B1 LENGTH:
TYPE: COLUMN COLUMN: Sean *Kirst*

BYLINE: SEAN *KIRST* POST-STANDARD COLUMNIST

A few days ago, Charlie Bailey picked up a ringing phone at his Baldwinsville home. The caller identified himself only as an elderly man. He wanted to express his sympathy for Bailey, who had gone public with his account of boyhood abuse by a Roman Catholic priest.

The caller said the same thing had happened to him, as a child, many years ago.

But he would not give Bailey his name or phone number.

The conversation ended. Bailey's caller went back to suffering alone.

His reluctance to seek help underlines a concern for national and local leaders in the movement for healing victims of clerical abuse: The overwhelming majority of allegations against priests or other church employees have come from children of the baby boom, children who grew up from the 1950s into the 1980s.

As for older Americans, most of them are keeping their horrors to themselves.

"In that generation, you didn't question the church," said Bailey, 52, coordinator of the Syracuse chapter of the Survivors Network of Those Abused by Priests, or SNAP. "I believe there's just so much shame and guilt and embarrassment."

Men and women born in the late 1930s or earlier were especially vulnerable to sexual predators.

Countless thousands of elderly Americans spent their childhoods in Catholic orphanages, seminaries or convents during the Great Depression, isolated from any way of seeking help.

Catholic parents were often immigrants or first-generation citizens, steeped in church rules of obedience.

Compound that with the clinical reality that abuse begets abuse—meaning that many of today's pedophile priests are part of a chain that started long ago—and logic would indicate that pre-World War II conditions made a fertile ground for molesting children.

If anything, said David Clohessy, the abuse in those years was probably much worse.

Even so, the number of reported allegations from that era remains low. Clohessy, 47, became national director of SNAP after he found the courage to go public with his own tale of abuse. Of the hundreds of victims he has met or counseled over the years, Clohessy estimates that only a small percentage came of age before World War II.

The memory of one victim is enough to bring Clohessy to tears. He recalled taking a phone call from an 86-year-old, a retired basketball coach. The man wanted help in writing a letter that would be added to his will. The letter would explain to his children what a priest had done to him.

"The guy called me out of the blue, and he had been living with this (alone) for decades and decades," Clohessy said. "He'd always been afraid that if people knew he'd been abused by a priest, that they wouldn't want their kids on his bas-ketball team."

The image haunts Clohessy, this vision of white-haired men and women who continue to hide their ordeals from their spouses and their children. The code of silence, Clohessy said, was much stronger in the America of 60 or 70 years ago. Mothers and fathers were afraid of challenging the church, and a child's word had little chance against the aura of a priest.

Even now, Clohessy said, that code of silence still holds sway.

"For a 70- to 80-year-old Catholic to deal with this is different than it is even for a 30- or 40-year-old Catholic, because it's two different worlds," said Teresa Secreti, assistance coordinator for the Roman Catholic Diocese of Syracuse, who said her "heart goes out" to that entire generation.

One major difference for elderly victims is that the priests who caused their pain have probably been dead for years. With no chance to bring about a reckon-ing, many victims might wonder why it's worth it to seek help.

"Because the truth will set you free," Clohessy said. "Because you can say to your children and your grandchildren, "This happened to me and this is how I suffered, and don't you dare stay silent if the same thing happens to you."

Danielle Cummings, spokeswoman for the diocese, agrees with Clohessy. She said Secreti is available to help any victims of abuse. That includes elderly men and women who were molested by priests, staff or other children in any orphan-age or institution, and "anybody who's been abused by a member of church per-sonnel."

"We want to help them," Cummings said of that older generation. "We want to hear their stories and up to now, we haven't heard their stories."

Both Clohessy and Cummings described speaking the truth as the first step toward real peace. As an example, Clohessy recalled a man he met in 1991, out-side a church in St. Louis, Mo. Clohessy and others from SNAP were handing out papers explaining their purpose. The man, tall and white-haired, stopped and read a leaflet.

"He looked at me, with tears in his eyes, and said, "This happened to me, too,'" Clohessy recalled.

The man's name was Bill Russell. "There are an awful lot of us with the same story to tell, if we wanted to tell it," said Russell, 74, who still lives in Missouri. In a phone interview Wednesday, he said he was molested as a child, by both a fam-ily member and a Methodist minister. For more than a half-century, Russell shared the burden with no one, including his wife.

Finally, to his great relief, he let his story out. But he knows that among his peers he is the exception. His generation endured the Great Depression, World War II, the Korean War. It consisted of men and women accustomed to quiet sacrifice, men and women taught that sharing your own trauma was unseemly.

Instead, as Russell learned, it's the only ray of hope.

Sean *Kirst* is a columnist with The Post-Standard. His columns appear Mondays, Wednesdays and Fridays. Call him at 470-6015 or e-mail him at citynews@syracuse.com

To find help

Elderly survivors of sexual abuse within the church are invited to a meeting of the local chapter of SNAP—Survivor Network of Those Abused by Priests—at 7 p.m. Friday, at the Lysander Town Hall. Detailed information on SNAP and its local chapters is available at www.survivorsnetwork.org

Survivors can also call Teresa Secreti, assistance coordinator for the Roman Catholic Diocese of Syracuse, who is available for confidential help and counseling at 470-1465.

PRIEST ABUSE VICTIM PLEADS FOR FULL DISCLOSURE LYSANDER MAN PLEADS FOR BISHOP TO REVEAL ALL 49 PRIESTS WHO ARE ACCUSED.

The Post-Standard
Saturday, *January 17*, 2004
EDITION: Final SECTION: Local PAGE: B6 LENGTH:

BYLINE: By Jennifer *Jacobs* Staff writer

Trembling and uncertain, Charles Bailey forced himself to step into a Roman Catholic church Friday for the first time in years to plead that the bishop reveal the names of 49 priests in the Syracuse diocese accused of sexual abuse in the last 50 years.

"How do you trust any priest until you know who the bad guys are?" said Bailey, of Lysander, who says he was raped more than 100 times by an Onondaga Hill priest in the 1960s. "There were five priests on the altar tonight. How do we know they aren't five of the 49?"

In the jaws of a brutal cold snap, about 22 people joined Bishop James Moynihan for his second solemn prayer service, "A Time of Healing," at Holy Family Church in Fairmount. A similar service was Oct. 30 at St. Mary Church in Oswego, and two more are planned in Oneida and Broome counties.

Bailey sat in the front row. His wife Susan wrapped an arm around his shoulders. He wept.

Bailey said that in 1961, when he was 10 years old, Rev. Thomas Neary promised him that sex would make him more holy. When he cried in pain, Baily said the priest told him to be quiet because his suffering was nothing compared to the pain of Jesus' crucifixion. Neary died on Sept. 17, 2001.

Bailey, now 52, reported the abuse to the Syracuse diocese in March. Diocesan officials have refused to discuss allegations against Neary; they offered counseling to Bailey.

During Friday's service, Moynihan fell to his knees and remained there for several minutes. "Each day I cannot help but remember that my brothers and sisters have something against me," he said, his voice gravelly but strong. "I'm here to say I repent of all the sins that have been committed. There's no doubt in my mind about the great harm that's been done."

Moynihan continued, his eyes downcast, "I also know I can hardly begin to make things right. For the victims, some things will never be right."

After the prayer service, Moynihan sat next to Bailey, who asked him to identify the 49 priests referred to in a letter the diocese distributed at Masses this month.

Moynihan shook his head. Since his first public comments about the scandal in February 2002, he has refused, saying church policy protects the accused as well as the victims.

Wendy Christopher, who said she belongs to a Catholic church in Warners, confronted Moynihan, saying it was a mistake to have covered up abuse.

ABOUT THE AUTHOR

I, Charles L. Bailey, Jr., am fifty-five years old. I am the husband of Susan, the father of four children, and the grandfather of eight. I was born and raised in Syracuse, New York, and remain there today. After high school, I went on to get my two-year degree in civil technology.

After college, I worked for a general contractor as an estimator, which involved calculating the quantities of material and labor to build buildings. I then worked for the local gas and electric company for the rest of my career. I worked in engineering in the nuclear fuel management department. While there, my job broadened in scope to include nuclear and fossil fuel management. I moved from there into the power control division, where I spent the remainder of my career. I advanced in position throughout the department until I reached the rank of shift supervisor of power operations. I had ultimate control of the high voltage power operations on a minute-by-minute basis, trying to preserve the integrity of the system and keep the lights on for all. After more than twenty-five years of service, I retired because of health problems.

I have been an activist in support of abuse victims for over four years now. I am the local leader of SNAP (Survivors Network of those Abused by Priests, www.snapnetwork.org). I was a breakout session leader in June 2005 in Chicago at the National SNAP Conference. I also provide a lot of one-on-one support of victims who are still too fragile to publicly come forward.

I have been guest speaker to Catholic groups, such as The Voice of the Faithful, Call To Action, Coalition of Concerned Catholics, and others. I attended the Sexual Betrayal and Scandal in the Catholic Church Seminar at the Mount Sinai Medical Center in New York City in November 2004, where I queried the panel about handling trust issues. I have testified before the New York State Senate hearings on childhood sexual abuse on two occasions, and I stood with Assemblywoman Margaret Markey when she announced her bill on childhood sexual abuse. I have been working with an FBI agent over the past couple of years, providing him with suspected abusers information. I met with our local district attorney, who was visibly moved by my personal account and has offered his help, trusting me with his cell and home phone numbers, telling me to call him anytime I feel it's needed. We have gotten a child sex abuse bill passed in the New York State assembly, and we await its passage in the New York Senate. I was invited to and attended the HBO premiere of *Twist of Faith* in June 2005 at HBO Studios in New York City. I was featured in the *Legislative Gazette* in May 2003.

I work with the local media to speak out for myself and for those who cannot speak out. I attend court appearances to support those who have difficulty standing alone.

978-0-595-40578-
0-595-40578-9

CPSIA information can be obtained at www.ICGtesting.com
Printed in the USA
BVOW08s0418260815

415044BV00001B/23/P

9 780595 405787